Educating Everyone

Drawing on the latest neuroscientific research and rooted in good practice, *Educating Everyone* presents the concept of Relational Inclusion, encouraging schools to reconsider their traditional perspectives on mental health and behaviour.

The authors pose thought-provoking questions about longstanding conventional approaches to behaviour management in schools that have remained largely unchanged since the inception of compulsory state education. They present a range of strategies that extend beyond the needs of individuals with complex requirements who are often isolated as a result of the misguided concept that they can be "taught" to conform. Relational Inclusion is advocated as an inclusive approach that can benefit all children and adults, fostering comprehension of the underlying causes behind behavioural challenges. This book provides an essential framework for responding to students' behaviour that has been tried and tested in real classrooms.

Schools play a pivotal role in teaching these essential skills and attitudes, and this accessible resource provides educators with valuable insights and practical strategies for creating a nurturing and supportive environment within school settings. It will appeal to educationalists across the educational sector, including headteachers and policy leaders as well as behaviour leads, classroom teachers, support staff, and anyone who works with children and young people.

Anthony Benedict is the CEO of Ambition Community Trust and the Executive Head Teacher of Tameside Pupil Referral Service.

Alan Braven has recently retired, but was the Executive Headteacher of Endeavour Federation which provides the majority of Manchester's specialist provision for SEMH pupils.

Educating Everyone

An Introduction to Relational Inclusion in Schools

Anthony Benedict and
Alan Braven

LONDON AND NEW YORK

Designed cover image: Anthony Benedict and Alan Braven, 2024

First published 2025
by Routledge
4 Park Square, Milton Park, Abingdon, Oxon OX14 4RN

and by Routledge
605 Third Avenue, New York, NY 10158

Routledge is an imprint of the Taylor & Francis Group, an informa business

© 2025 Anthony Benedict and Alan Braven

The right of Anthony Benedict and Alan Braven to be identified as authors of this work has been asserted in accordance with sections 77 and 78 of the Copyright, Designs and Patents Act 1988.

All rights reserved. No part of this book may be reprinted or reproduced or utilised in any form or by any electronic, mechanical, or other means, now known or hereafter invented, including photocopying and recording, or in any information storage or retrieval system, without permission in writing from the publishers.

Trademark notice: Product or corporate names may be trademarks or registered trademarks, and are used only for identification and explanation without intent to infringe.

British Library Cataloguing-in-Publication Data
A catalogue record for this book is available from the British Library

ISBN: 9781032874845 (hbk)
ISBN: 9781032874838 (pbk)
ISBN: 9781003532866 (ebk)

DOI: 10.4324/9781003532866

Typeset in Galliard
by Deanta Global Publishing Services, Chennai, India

To
Elsie, Eliza, and Eli
And, of course, my dad, who never got to read it

To
My mam and dad who would have been immensely proud, and surprised
And all those who throughout my life have inspired me

This book wouldn't exist without the thousands of children and staff we've taught and worked with. We didn't always get it right, but we'd never have got as far as we have without meeting all of you along the way. Thank you for letting us be part of your story. This book is for all of you and for all of those of you we're yet to meet.

Contents

About the Authors   *viii*
Authors' Note   *x*

    Introduction: It's Time for Change   1
1   How Did We Get Here?   13
2   Guiding Principles   33
3   Relationships, Relationships, Relationships   56
4   Don't Try to Fix Me   76
5   The Lost Children   101
6   Words   125
7   Fostering a Culture of Compassion   139
8   System Change and the Golden Thread   162

Epilogue   *187*
Acknowledgements   *189*
Index   *191*

About the Authors

Anthony has been a qualified teacher for 27 years. He started his career as an English teacher and has worked in five different authorities and held senior roles, predominantly in secondary education, in six different schools. He is the CEO of a brand-new multi-academy trust which has been designed around the principles of Relational Inclusion.

Roughly five years ago he left mainstream education for alternative provision. It seemed to him that the school system was "losing" too many children, even when some of them were hidden in plain sight. He had recognised that if children were tired or hungry or scared then they weren't going to be able to learn. He had a simple idea that if schools could meet these very basic needs, it might help prevent some of the so-called behavioural problems that were so prevalent and seemed to escalate so quickly. After his first day in charge of a Pupil Referral Unit he realised that he needed to unlearn all he had previously thought about how schools work and start again. He fell down what he likes to refer to as a trauma and attachment rabbit hole and hasn't looked back since.

He has become unashamedly evangelical about what he has learnt in terms of neuroscience and childhood brain development and cannot believe that anyone who wants to work in schools or with children isn't provided with this as prerequisite training before they are taught how to teach.

He has spent the last four years developing Relational Inclusion and has worked with anyone and everyone who is prepared to listen including the Violence Reduction Unit, the police, Manchester University, and of course primary, secondary, and special schools and PRUs.

He is absolutely on a mission to change the world.

Alan has been a teacher for 35 years, with a significant portion of his career spent in senior leadership roles. He began his journey as a maths teacher, working with some of the most complex young people in London and Manchester. From the outset, Alan chose a path that diverged from the norm, opting to work in schools facing challenging circumstances rather than pursuing easier, more conventional roles. This decision defined his career, even though it meant navigating schools that were often at risk of closure due to the difficulties they faced.

Throughout his career, Alan has been driven by a desire to "make a difference." As a young head of maths, he pioneered a progressive approach to teaching, moving away from rigid traditional methods to embrace mixed-ability teaching, using a scheme of work pioneered by the Inner London Education Authority. His commitment to finding better ways to support working-class children has been central to his work.

Around 12 years ago, Alan transitioned into special education leadership, a move that deepened his understanding of how to support children with complex needs. He quickly recognised that traditional systems of rewards and sanctions were insufficient. Over time, he became passionate about the neuroscience behind student behaviour and learning, and he has since worked to implement systems that better address the needs of all children.

Alan is currently focused on establishing a new multi-academy trust grounded in the principles of Relational Inclusion. His belief that there is always a better way to support students has been the guiding force of his career, undeterred by those who advocate for a more rigid approach to student behaviour.

Anthony and Alan are both committed to making positive change. If you want to be a part of this change and would like one (or both) of them to support your school or academy, please get in touch. You can contact them through the Ambition Community Trust website.

Authors' Note

Alan and Anthony have worked collaboratively for the last five years. It began with a shared interest in how to best support the children in their respective SEMH schools and Pupil Referral Units whilst also considering what was missing in mainstream schools.

As they worked, they were developing Relational Inclusion – although they didn't know it and hadn't a name for it yet. Their collaboration led to the creation of Ambition Community Trust – a brand-new multi-academy trust – a series of staff and school training packages, and several pilots with both primary and secondary schools.

When Alan asked Anthony if he thought it might be a good idea to capture what they had been doing in a book, it made perfect sense. They set about writing the book that you now hold in your hands. Having never written a book, they weren't quite sure how it would work. How do an English teacher and a maths teacher write a book about changing approaches to whole-school behaviour? How do two people write with one voice?

They discussed an outline and wrote it down. Then Anthony wrote a bit and sent it to Alan and Alan wrote a bit and sent it back to Anthony. They swapped stories and soon realised that they shared a ridiculous amount of teaching and leadership experiences. So much of their journey to this point had been so similar that it was uncanny. They decided that instead of telling two stories, with two voices, from two authors, they would try and merge their experiences. And they think it worked quite well.

Although all the events discussed in this book are true, the narrator is a fictional character made up of bits of both of them. They have tried to avoid using names – the people in this book purposely don't relate to anyone specifically – the story is more about the lessons Alan and Anthony have learnt along the way. They very much hope that this book will be a catalyst for the change the education system is in desperate need of.

Introduction
It's Time for Change

Often it appears easier to wait for change than to be the one responsible for change. Afterall, who are we? Are there not more important people, more influential people in the world than us? Barack Obama (2008) said, "Change will not come if we wait for some other person or some other time. We are the ones we've been waiting for. We are the change that we seek." And I think this is true. Maybe it's my age, but of late, increasingly I find myself sitting in more and more meetings and listening to people talk about what we might do differently and discuss changes that need to take place, only for nothing to happen. I used to say nothing and nod along, but I have decided to change my approach. If we don't voice our thoughts, then we can't complain when nothing changes. This book is about change. Change is good and change is necessary, so let's stop talking and let's start doing. Let's be *the change we seek*.

***

Yeats talked about concentric gyres (Mitchell, n.d.). He said that historical eras overlap, one ending as the next one begins. He believed that these gyres fell into roughly two-thousand-year periods and whilst one dominates, the other is always implied and weakly present.

I believe that we are living in a transitional point in history. We are living in the overlap of gyres that Yeats may have been referring to. Change is happening but not quite quickly enough. Old ideas merge with new thinking and no-one is quite sure which way we're heading. Consequently, everyone is either treading water or drowning and it seems that there is no space for swimming freely.

For now, many of us in education feel that we're sinking fast. There has been a global pandemic. Schools are struggling – really struggling – and

DOI: 10.4324/9781003532866-1

they're not sure what to struggle with first: Lack of funding, "naughty" children, attendance, persistent absenteeism, exclusions, lack of SEN support, pressure on results, teachers leaving the profession in droves, teachers staying in the profession who need to leave, and AI and the very real possibility that *Terminator* might not be a total work of fiction.

Educational thinking is divided. Two camps are emerging: The *Behaviourists* and the *Relationalists*. The Behaviourists believe in meeting the "behaviour crisis" with strict behaviour policies: They believe in silent corridors and very clear, non-negotiable, "red" lines. They offer a transparent, albeit sometimes inflexible, tariff-driven behaviour system, in which clear punishments are matched to specific behaviours. They have a *one-size-fits-all* approach which unfortunately ultimately sees those children who *don't fit the model* permanently excluded. The problem with this method is that these children must go somewhere. Is it okay to just pass the buck? I am not fickle. I once believed in and applied this model myself.

But aren't all children ours to care for, to nurture, to take responsibility for? And don't they all become our problem if they simply feed the PRU to prison pipeline?

There are then the *Relationalists*. These are the group who believe we can run schools differently. They apply a more student-centred approach and incorporate elements of socio-cultural theory. They believe in neuroscience, in the impact of trauma and attachment, that one size doesn't fit all, that red lines don't work. That relationships and inclusive practice are the way forward. They have swapped behaviour policies for relational policies.

The world is suddenly becoming a very different place and I'm certain people will look back on this period of time and wonder why on earth we did what we did. They will certainly question why we treated young people struggling with their mental health in such a poor way, in the same way that we look back at the way racism in schools or Section 28 were accepted as "the way things were."

Whichever camp you sit in, what is clear is we haven't yet cracked behaviour. If we had there would be an off-the-shelf package which everyone would have bought, learned, and applied, and there would be no more "naughty" children. The harsh reality is that there isn't a silver bullet. What is also clear is that our current behaviourist approaches don't work (if the aim is to change behaviours). Detention halls are full of the same children night after night after night. Often behaviour policies work for children who would behave anyway and have little impact, and sometimes the opposite effect, on those who do need support with managing their emotions. Perhaps the only question, going forward, is should some schools be allowed to excuse themselves from dealing with "challenging" children by excluding them, adding to their trauma, and then expecting others to "pick up the pieces," or do we all take some responsibility? This way **all** schools could be judged on how well they cater for **all** children, not just those who are compliant.

As Lori Desautels states in her book, *Connections over Compliance*:

> Many current school discipline procedures are forms of punishment that work best with the students who need them the least. With our most difficult students, the current discipline models don't change their behavior, often escalating the challenges and problems by unintentionally reactivating those students' stress response systems.
>
> (Desautels, 2024)

It's time for change, and although it doesn't always feel that way, change is good. This book explores some of the changes that we could make for the good of everyone. It isn't a step-by-step handbook. It isn't a magic wand (I really wish it was). We hope that what you find among these pages is help in seeing behaviour through a different lens and understanding different strategies you can then apply.

Relational Inclusion must not be seen as "another new initiative." It cannot be "done by Christmas"; it is not a one-day INSET that staff complete only to move onto the next thing.

It must become the golden thread which knits a school's community, culture, and ethos together. It is not a quick fix; it will take time and conscious effort. If nurtured sensibly, it will evolve to become the heartbeat of the school.

Adopting a relational and inclusive approach is not rocket science. Some of the most effective staff will already be applying some of these techniques. This book will provide the glue to bring current research and thinking together and apply it consistently to make real change.

The Start of an Idea

Let me take you back 20 years or so. Most classrooms had whiteboards. I was proud to still have a blackboard. The first interactive boards were starting to appear. Data was completed on a separate computer usually in a stock cupboard at the end of the day, often a Friday. Wireless keyboards and mice were a new kind of magic. Work was saved on disks.

The school system became obsessed with putting children in visual, audio, or kinaesthetic learning boxes.

And we had a problem with year 10 boys. To be more precise we had a problem with about eight year 10 boys. They were taking up everyone's time and ruining everyone's lessons when they were present. When they weren't in school, we had an attendance problem. Whilst in conversation with my headteacher, I heard myself saying: "What you need to do is ..."

Back then I was young and enthusiastic. My head was full of ideas about how we could change the face of education, how we could change and improve the world. Sometimes my mouth operated before my brain. With hindsight, the outcome possibly wouldn't have been any different, but I might have thought through my idea a little more clearly.

My idea was to put all the boys together, in the same form, with a teacher who "understood" them. That teacher could act as a mentor and put "some kind of support" in place and act as a kind of buffer for the rest of the school. You can probably see where this is going.

The head said, "That is a great idea. And I've got just the person to do it."

I can't remember the exact details of the rest. I like to think that, with innocent naivety, I said, "Who?"

As you'd expect, the reply was, "You." And that was that.

My only regret was that I lost my first ever proper form. I had nurtured them from year 7 "babies" and was really looking forward to taking them through to year 11 and supporting them to grow and develop. They were a great form group, and we had a brilliant relationship. It was not to be. From the next half term, I was to have a form of ten of the "most challenging" year 10 boys. To be fair, at least three of them had been in my form anyway. With all honesty, the three weren't a problem for me – which is quite an "annoying teacher" thing to say. With hindsight, it's probably why the head wanted me to have this form.

I had half an idea of how this new form would work. It wasn't based on any theory or research. Schools weren't so hot on such things back then. I worked with my gut feelings and my instinct.

My idea was that we would establish a really clear set of rules and boundaries. And I meant this sincerely. We talked together about how we needed to operate, what our worries and concerns were, and how we could work together to manage them. We established an open and honest culture.

We spent the first five to ten minutes of form time talking. No agenda. We would talk about the weekend, the day ahead, anything interesting that had come up. I had been selected to have the first "new and interactive whiteboard" so they spent the next five minutes playing on that.

One of the issues with the boys was their "uncontrollable" behaviour around school. They seemed to "lose it" at the drop of a hat. They had meltdowns and tantrums; they swore at staff and tended to throw chairs and tables.

We talked about how they felt and their triggers, and I asked them if they were able to predict when this might happen or at least when it was starting to happen. They said they could. I said, "How about if, when you feel it happening, you walk out of the class, without swearing or throwing things, and come to me?"

They were worried that they would get in further trouble for walking out, or fall into conflict with a teacher and then the situation would escalate. I explained that I would clear it with all their teachers. Their class teachers were, in fact, delighted that the boys could leave their room without having to be sent out. Before long, staff used this as a form of behaviour management: "Don't you think you would be better off going to see your form tutor?"

I made it clear that the only condition was that they were not to take advantage of this. I explained that if they felt themselves losing control, they were fine to come to me at any time. If, however, they just didn't like the lesson, that wasn't a good enough reason. They agreed. I also said that they would have to sit with whichever class I was teaching, and they needed to not disrupt my lesson. I said I would work with them and talk to them, but they had to respect my teaching as well.

I'd like to say we had behaviour charts and reward ladders and all sorts of fancy systems. But we didn't. All we had was a safe place for the child to come and an opportunity to talk about their problems, sometimes over a cup of coffee. That was it.

And guess what? It worked. By giving these students the time to be heard, by listening to their needs, and by providing them with a framework in which they could succeed, their needs were better met. In fact, it worked so well that the following year I had the whole group for 16 lessons per week. Most of the staff were very happy with the arrangement, and the pupils were enjoying school (mostly). It created some other problems; as their attendance improved some staff were a little disgruntled that they were virtually always present. It meant that pretty much every lesson I taught, one or two of them would appear. We'd have a quick conversation, and they'd sit at the back of my class, and I'd have something for them to do. To be fair to them, it had a really positive impact on all of my other classes. If anyone started to misbehave, one of the year 10 boys (who I imagine had quite big reputations around and outside of school) would quietly explain that they needed to behave themselves as "sir was alright."

When I taught them for 16 lessons per week and we were all getting a bit too stressed, they, or I, would suggest story time and they would happily sit quietly for half an hour and listen to me reading them a story. And this is something we often forget. However big they are, however difficult their lives might be, they are still children. And all children love the soothing tone of a well-read story.

Back then I probably thought I was some kind of teaching wizard with magical skills of classroom control. Clearly, I wasn't. I could unpick everything we did and explain the theory and research behind why it worked, but that is the job of this book.

They say everything happens for a reason. They say everything we do sets us up for what we will become. Though I didn't know it at the time, with that group of boys, the seeds of what would become *Relational Inclusion* were firmly planted.

Many years later I tried a similar, more refined project as headteacher. This time there was a bit more analysis. In-school data was telling me that roughly 10 percent of my students were causing 90 percent of my problems.

I decided that I needed to separate these students from the main population, not as a punishment but as a way of helping them engage and avoid suspension or exclusion. Obviously, the irony is not lost as I write this now, for I was still isolating them from their peers.

I created what we now call an "Internal Alternative Provision." Once again, I tried to identify staff who were able to work with "these kind of children" (not me this time). I adjusted their curriculum. I included visits from the police and ex-gangsters (not to pigeonhole them or anything). I had moderate success.

When I moved out of mainstream education, I had a vague notion that if children were hungry or tired or cold or scared they would struggle to engage with learning. I was ready to change the world. Then the stark reality hit me. I had 100 children who had all been permanently excluded from mainstream education. I couldn't put them in detention. I couldn't isolate them. I couldn't suspend them. I couldn't permanently exclude them. Shouting wouldn't work. They were causing damage of £80,000 a year to the building. There had to be another way to do this...

Breaking the Behaviour Cycle

> There comes a point where we need to stop just pulling people out of the river. We need to go up stream and find out why they're falling in.
>
> (Desmond Tutu)

Even when I was at school, different families had different reputations. Everyone knew who the tough kids were, we knew who the bullies were, and we knew who the "naughty" children were. Generally poor behaviour ran through family lines.

As a teacher, the first thing I did when I got my new class list was scan for familiar surnames. Probably, because of automatic negative thinking, I wasn't searching for the "good" children. I was looking for familiar surnames of "naughty" children. I used to think that if their older siblings had been through the school and didn't know how to behave themselves, chances were that the younger version would be equally as bad or worse. The same applies for older teachers who had taught the parents and knew exactly what to look out for in their children.

When a recognisable "rogue" surname was identified, it was usually accompanied by that "sinking" feeling. It was likely that this class was going to be tricky. There was a battle ahead.

**Automatic Negative Thoughts (ANTS)
or Negative Thinking Patterns**

When, out of the blue, your boss asks to see you, what is your first thought? Generally, you don't think you are being summoned to receive a pay rise. You get that awful sinking feeling in your stomach and presume you have done something wrong, and you are in some kind of trouble. This is an example of automatic negative thinking and can be traced back to our survival instinct.

> The brains of humans and other animals contain a mechanism that is designed to give priority to bad news. By shaving a few hundredths of a second from the time needed to detect a predator, this circuit improves the animal's odds of living long enough to reproduce.
>
> (Kahneman, 2012)
>
> When we were hunters (and sometimes hunted) these instincts served us well. In the modern world, these thoughts can flood our minds like an army of tiny ANTs and can generate emotions such as anxiety, sadness, frustration, guilt, anger, or unworthiness. We sometimes forget or overlook the fact that children also experience these. See Figure 0.1.

As I became a more experienced teacher, I began to wonder why this happened. Why did bad behaviour travel through families? Surely this was the parents' fault; they should know better, shouldn't they?

In 2011, Ken Clarke, the then-justice secretary, said:

> There is an urgent need to stop reoffending among a feral underclass. He went on to say punishment alone was "not enough" and individuals and families familiar with the justice system … hadn't been changed by their past punishments.
>
> (Lewis et al., 2011)

Which made me think of "let them eat cake," the misquote attributed to Marie Antoinette, and "beatings will continue until morale improves" [unknown].

I realised that something was very wrong. At the very least I had fallen victim of deficit thinking. I was subconsciously blaming students and their families for behavioural challenges. This was not good enough. I do not believe there is a "feral underclass" – this sounds Dickensian and discriminatory. It's offensive.

I've spent most of my career working with children labelled as "naughty." As this book unfolds, I will argue that children don't choose to behave badly. There is something else going on. How do we break the behaviour cycle?

I also noticed that the so-called naughty children behaved very differently if their physical environment changed. When I was a deputy

Figure 0.1 Negative Thinking Patterns.

headteacher and staff were struggling, I often removed children from class and brought them to my office. Here their behaviour was completely different. They were happy to talk sensibly and complete small jobs such as sorting folders and running errands. They also then behaved totally differently in my lesson. They began to comply.

I understand that spending time with children and young people to build relationships is vitally important, but this is only part of the solution, and relationships alone won't ultimately change behaviour and emotional responses. These children might be "fine for me," but they were still unsettled around the building, they still caused problems in lessons, they still weren't learning, and they were often causing major problems outside of school. As I reflect on these children today, I know that shortly after leaving school, many of them received prison sentences of varying lengths for a variety of crimes – some petty, many violent, in the worst case, murder. The longer I stayed in teaching, the more pupils would happily tell me that I "taught their parent." If I didn't already know, the resemblance was suddenly obvious.

I came into teaching to change the world, to make it a better place. More explicitly, I wanted to change the world for young people. And for some of them I was failing.

Then I read about epigenetics.

> Epigenetics is an emerging area of scientific research that shows how environmental influences—children's experiences—actually affect the expression of their genes. This means the old idea that genes are "set in stone" has been disproven. Nature vs. Nurture is no longer a debate.
>
> Centre on the developing child, Harvard university (Center on the Developing Child at Harvard University, n.d.)

In really simple terms, it used to be believed that some genes were passed down from parent to child whilst some were not. Epigenetics suggests that humans have far fewer genes than other animals, and actually they are all passed down but, excuse my poetic license, they are like switches which are either turned on or off. This means that if a parent has experienced or is living with trauma, or a mother experiences trauma during pregnancy, the trauma is likely to be passed to the child.

Gabor Mate was born in Budapest, Hungry. Nazi invasion was imminent. He describes how, in his first months of life, his mother couldn't stop him from crying. She took him to the doctor and the doctor replied, "All the Jewish babies are crying." Although mothers were desperately trying to keep their fear from their children, the trauma was being passed down, genetically.

Epigenetics and Rats

In 2004 a study was carried out with rats (Weaver et al., 2004). It had been noted that some rat mothers extensively licked and groomed their pups, whilst others ignored their pups. Licking in this way has been likened to love and affection. Pups that received this "affection" during the first weeks of their lives grew up to be happy and calm. The pups which were ignored and didn't receive "affection" grew to be anxious and were more prone to disease (licking rat pups: The genetics of nurture). It was also noted that pups who were nurtured by licking went on to lick their pups. Possibly unsurprisingly, pups who were ignored went on to ignore their pups.

The study was developed further. Once born, some of the pups were swapped before the nurturing began. So, pups whose mothers didn't lick were given to licking mothers and vice-versa. The characteristics of the pups changed. Those who were now nurtured by licking, grew up to be happy and calm. They went on to lick their pups.

The pups born by licking mothers but nurtured by mothers who didn't lick grew to be more anxious and showed signs of stress hormones. They didn't nurture their own pups by licking.

Epigenetics and Mice

In 2013 a study was carried out with mice, cherry blossom, and electric shocks. The mice were placed near cherry blossom and given an electric shock. Not surprisingly the mice associated the smell of cherry blossom with electric shocks and became fearful of it as a result.

What made the experiment even more fascinating was that the children of the mice experimented on and the grandchildren of the mice experimented on were also fearful of the smell. This was referred to as *epigenetic inheritance* (Geddes, 2013).

Stephi Wagner suggests that "Pain travels through families until someone is ready to heal it." It is possible that this is one reason why difficult behaviour seems to be a common thread in certain families. If this is the case, no amount of punishment and no amount of enforced discipline will support a change in behaviour. If we are going to *break the behaviour cycle*, wouldn't it be sensible to find the root cause, instead of trying to address the symptoms? "We need to go up stream and find out why they're falling in."

Epigenetics certainly raises some interesting questions. Is there a difference between learned behaviour and "epigenetic" inherited behaviour? What impact is intergenerational trauma having on our young people and how does this show itself in the classroom, the playground, and in society? We have had a global pandemic, we are living with war, we are starting to recognise and address inherent racism.

If, as a society, we are aware of all these issues, what support are we providing? How are we adapting our practice? Ignorance is not an excuse.

References

Desautels, L. L. (2024). *Connections over compliance: Rewiring our perceptions of discipline*. Wyatt-MacKenzie Publishing.

Center on the Developing Child at Harvard University. (n.d.). *Epigenetics and child development: How children's experiences affect their genes*. https://developingchild.harvard.edu/resources/what-is-epigenetics-and-how-does-it-relate-to-child-development/

Geddes, L. (2013, December 1). *Fear of a smell can be passed down several generations*. New Scientist. https://www.newscientist.com/article/dn24677-fear-of-a-smell-can-be-passed-down-several-generations/

Kahneman, D. (2012). *Thinking, fast and slow*. Penguin.

Lewis, P., Taylor, M., & Ball, J. (2011). *Kenneth Clarke blames English riots on a 'broken penal system'*. The Guardian. https://www.theguardian.com/uk/2011/sep/05/kenneth-clarke-riots-penal-system

Mitchell, P. I. *Yeats' view of history*. Dallas Baptist University. https://www.dbu.edu/mitchell/world-literature-ii/yeatshis.html#:~:text=Yeats%20conceptualized%20history%20as%20a,always%20implied%20and%20weakly%20present.

Obama, B. (2008, February 5). Chicago, Illinois, speech after winning the Super Tuesday Primaries. http://obamaspeeches.com/E02-Barack-Obama-Super-Tuesday-Chicago-IL-February-5-2008.htm

Weaver, I. C. G., Cervoni, N., Champagne, F. A., D'Alessio, A. C., Sharma, S., Seckl, J. R., Dymov, S., Szyf, M., & Meaney, M. J. (2004). Epigenetic programming by maternal behavior. *Nature Neuroscience, 7*(8), 847–854.

Chapter 1

How Did We Get Here?

We build walls to protect ourselves. We then forget that we have become safe, but we keep the walls anyway. Sometimes we build more. Maybe it's for security. Maybe we just don't notice them anymore. Maybe they are just an excuse. Sometimes we need to knock the walls down and have a good look around. We must remember why we built them in the first place. Then, just maybe, we need to try to do things differently. Otherwise, as Margaret Atwood (1985) said: "A rat in a maze is free to go anywhere as long as it stays inside the maze." This chapter will explore some of the historical walls we have built around education.

***

I'm really good at shouting. I've got a really loud, aggressive voice, and I can switch into *bellow mode* in an instant. I'm only little, and I've been blessed with a face that looks like it had a really hard paper round (I didn't). I've a shaven head, and I'm tattooed. On more than one occasion, a stranger in a pub has asked if they shared a cell with me (they didn't).

When I worked in South Yorkshire (Royston, an ex-mining community, where everyone had been an extra in the film version of *Kes*), I shouted at a boy in year 10 so loudly that he said, after things (well, I) had calmed down:

"Sir, you shouted so loud I nearly sh*t misen."

And I was quite proud of my achievement.

Several years later, I moved to a school in Salford. Shouting was by now a pretty well-embedded part of my classroom management and behaviour control routine… until I shouted at a year 10 girl, and she said, "Is that the best you've got? That's nothing compared to what my dad does."

DOI: 10.4324/9781003532866-2

And that made me think and reflect and wonder what on earth I was trying to achieve.

In 2024 the BBC published an article with the heading "The School Where Teachers Never Shout at Children." It further explains that "teachers are told never to shout at children who misbehave" which suggests this is a remarkable and unusual thing (Jessup, 2024). I think it is worth reflecting on this for a minute. Where else in society is it okay to walk up to someone and shout at them because you don't like the way they are behaving? There are schools that say, through policy, "we don't shout," but in my experience many staff still do.

This idea of shouting is an interesting concept. Why do we think it's okay to shout at children? Why do we think shouting will change behaviour? Common sense suggests that such an approach only teaches us that it's okay for big people to shout at little people.

I can't count the number of times I've seen staff standing nose to nose with children and young people, screaming in their faces, spit flying the short distance between.

I think back to my PGCE days. We all had to do a reflective project after our first teaching practice. One pair presented whilst wearing t-shirts stating "I shout at kids," highlighting the ridiculous nature of our practice all those years ago. It didn't stop us from becoming the next generation of shouters.

You see, back then we weren't really taught behaviour management. I remember being taught (as a baby teacher) not to smile at a class until Christmas (which I dutifully ignored). I wasn't taught about neuroscience or the developing brain or attachment or trauma. I was taught through the "sink or swim" method. By that I mean I pretty much got dropped into a classroom and had to survive. So largely I adapted to the way I had been taught, which was based on fairly inconsistent discipline, threats of detention which weren't always followed up, and, of course, shouting.

The limited behaviour training I did receive consisted of wedging myself in the door jamb so that I could simultaneously see all the pupils arriving from the corridors as well as those who had already entered the classroom. Then, meerkat-esque, I'd stand in front of the class constantly scanning the room so that I could see what was going on everywhere whilst the scowl on my face hopefully passed on the message that "I had everything under control" *and* "I wouldn't tolerate any nonsense." Nobody ever explained quite what I was supposed to do if I did see a pupil doing something wrong. There was a well-understood rule that pupils were supposed to do as they were told, and if they didn't, they were to blame. If raising my voice didn't work, then I obviously needed to shout a bit louder. There was a general agreement that competent teachers should get the class quiet before raising their voices so that they were not shouting over the pupils. There were some teachers whose mere footsteps in the corridor could silence a class. And all the new teachers watched in awe, wondering how they could gain that superpower.

I suppose somewhere down the line, I learnt that magic and became one of those teachers. I could walk into a chaotic classroom where children were shouting and throwing things and seemed generally out of control, raise an eyebrow, and silence fell without a word being spoken. It wasn't magic of course. It was based on relationships. The children knew me, they knew I listened to them, I cared for them, I was there to help, and there was mutual respect because of this.

Now don't get me wrong, at every point in my career, there has been a class or a student who has taken me to pieces. As teachers, we are always learning; just when we think we've nailed it, there is a new situation that takes us by surprise. In more recent times, I had real issues with a year 7 boy. He looked like a Dickensian street urchin. He was malnourished and small and wild. I said he was feral (a phrase I am not proud of and would never use about a child now). I simply could not manage him. He would run, he would jolt, he would climb out of windows, and I couldn't get near him. You could spend a whole morning chasing him.

And then I met a member of staff who was going to change my approach forever. She was new to the school and ran our inclusion room. She didn't chase him. She didn't shout at him. Within five minutes of being in her presence, he trotted alongside her like a little lost puppy. This was new "witchcraft," and I wanted to know more.

In my early career, schools didn't talk about managing or understanding behaviour; we "dealt with bad behaviour." I remember the trainees being given various scenarios and being asked, "what if...?" After one lesson observation, when a child had not handed in their homework, my tutor asked what I could have done differently. I was advised to "come down hard" on them as this was the "thin end of the wedge!" If it was not "dealt with" swiftly and harshly, then clearly, I would encounter many problems in the future, and basically my whole teaching career would be under threat.

I think all early career teachers live partly in fear. They worry about the balance of power and only ever having just enough control, about the fragility of their position and what will happen if they suddenly lose the tiny bit of perceived control they have.

Many of the trainees on my course had successful personal experiences of life in schools. They had rarely been in trouble with teachers, they had often been in the top ability streams, and they had little experience with poor behaviour. They were often from a more privileged background and had limited understanding of the needs of pupils from working-class families. They simply had no concept that some parents had several jobs, to try to keep things ticking along, and still struggled to feed their families and pay their bills.

In those early years of my career, I once confided in a senior teacher, as I was concerned about the progress that a particular pupil was making and their inability to focus on their learning. The advice was clear: "My dear, don't worry, our job is just to try to civilise these children."

That same year I had a career-defining moment. I had a class with "one of those students in." I was struggling. In every lesson that she was present, there was a problem. On one particular day, she had a total meltdown. She was screaming and throwing chairs. Some of the children were running for cover, some were delighting in winding her up even further, and some were asking, in the way only children can ask, "What are you going to do?" The problem was, I honestly didn't know what to do. I had no idea why she was behaving the way she was, and I had no idea how I could help. All sorts of thoughts were going through my mind. At the top of the list was every teacher's nightmare: Had I finally lost control? If I didn't do something very soon about this behaviour then it would escalate, it would become contagious and spread across all my classes like wildfire, my reputation would be ruined, and I would not be able to teach or control a class ever again.

There is nothing in teacher training that suggests anything like this might happen and certainly no guidance for what to do when it does. I was thoroughly unprepared for an event of this magnitude, and yet this is something that many teachers will experience in their careers.

I used every skill I had and, most importantly I didn't give up. Eventually, I succeeded in getting her outside the classroom. She was shouting and screaming and calling me all the names under the sun. I tried my best to remain calm and talk to her about what she had done and to explain that such behaviour was unacceptable. When she started to calm down, she shouted at me, "It's alright for you, you haven't just been raped by your father for the hundredth time!" I was floored. How is a teacher supposed to respond to that?

The point of this example is that my teacher training and early school experience had not prepared me for or given me any strategies to deal with this "bad" behaviour. No amount of raising my voice, shouting, or being clear about the "rules" would have changed the situation for the better. What did become very clear to me, at that moment, was that there had to be a better way.

My instinct to help was strong. I became a teacher because I wanted to help children, to make their world a better place, not to shout at them. Instead of asking for her to be punished and excluded, I chose to listen to her. I couldn't change her awful experience, I couldn't "fix" things, and I couldn't take away the pain.

I have no idea what happened to that girl over the years, but I doubt that the intervening years have taken away her pain and hurt. What I do know is that, at that point in my career, I understood that there was no set of rules anywhere that could have helped me with that incident. I was absolutely clear in my thinking that this wasn't personal and that she didn't wake up thinking, "How am I going to behave badly today?"

I also realised that it wasn't about me and my fear of the potential to lose control. This was all about the child, and I needed to better understand how to help her and others like her, no matter what their background or trauma.

I suppose that what I felt then, instinctively in my gut, has become the key to Relational Inclusion. I now **know** that these extreme behaviours, in fact many of our behaviours, are not a conscious choice. All behaviour **is** telling us something, if only we take the time to look. If a child could do better, I firmly believe that they would – but I didn't know the evidence behind this in those days. We (the teaching profession) need to know the neuroscience. I will pick this up later in the book, but it's important to state here and now, I am not making excuses for poor behaviour, I am not suggesting that choices made don't need to be addressed. I am stating that it's important to know and understand the emotions being experienced behind the behaviours. Teachers are not and should not be therapists or counsellors, but we should know the research. We should understand how the brain develops in children and how the body and nervous system operate.

If I don't sleep properly or eat properly, or I am scared, then I can't think properly, and this affects my moods, which in turn affects my behaviour. That's a basic understanding of how human beings work.

Why we aren't applying this in our classrooms as basic practice is a mystery.

As I've said, I was very good at shouting. Fortunately, by chance, and not to sound contradictory, I was also good at building relationships, creating warmth, and allowing children to feel seen and heard (when I wasn't shouting).

Post-Covid schools are a very different animal compared to the schools I learnt to teach in. I think more and more children are experiencing life like the girl I mentioned in Salford. Shouting doesn't work. Compliance behaviour systems don't work.

So, how have schools changed in the intervening years? Have they become more, or less, able to cope with incidents of poor behaviour? What happens now when a child is in crisis? How do schools manage this situation? How do we make our schools better places for all children and deal with all behaviours without resorting to exclusion?

There has been a very recent trend in schools to enforce ever stricter rules and to control every aspect of the child's life in school. Some schools proudly boast of having a "zero-tolerance" approach to "bad" behaviour and they vie to be stricter and more inflexible than their competitors. Schools have everything from silent corridors and school chants to mandated arrangements of pens and stationery on the desk and endless routines to "control" children. Headteachers, on opening evenings, have been heard to proudly announce, "If you don't like my rules, don't send your child to my school." And why wouldn't school leaders behave in this way? If Ofsted outcomes are anything to go by, this is the most successful approach. Parents are chomping at the bit to send their children to "behaviourist" schools and all is well in education land. We have had a head of Ofsted who has advocated this very approach and a behaviour Tsar who goes even further in ridiculing attempts to create a better school experience for all children.

It seems the answer is clear: All schools should adopt the same approach and then our problems will be solved. Schools are just factories, after all. Standardise the machine, fine-tune the robots. But as we know, schools are not factories. Children are not products. This approach does not meet the needs of all children. The evidence is overwhelming. These "behaviourist" schools routinely suspend and exclude children who do not (or cannot) comply with their strict rules far more than other schools. They have in-school "units" and "isolation booths" where children are taught separately from others until they "learn" to behave.

What do these schools mean by "zero tolerance" and what does it mean in practice? Does it mean the rest of us somehow tolerate bad behaviour? If a school has a zero-tolerance approach to bullying, what do they do when it occurs? Clearly, they don't tolerate it, so that must mean that the child is either excluded or given a severe punishment. The irony is that despite zero-tolerance policies, bullying still occurs in schools. So-called "bad behaviour" still occurs in schools. Is there any evidence that shows that a zero-tolerance approach leads to fewer incidents of bullying or that the child has a better or worse experience in school? I have never worked in a school that tolerates bullying or bad behaviour. And if these children are excluded, where do they then go?

> While framed in "positive language" [schools] remain based on this underlying principle: Do as you are told or we will need to punish you. If that continues not to work, we will banish you.
> (Desautels, 2020)

Data suggests that schools are indeed "banishing" children at an alarming level. The most recent published data shows that permanent exclusions and suspensions in schools are rising dramatically. Department for Education data published in November 2023 showed that there were 3,104 permanent exclusions in the autumn term of 2022/23, a 48% rise in the number from the autumn term of the year before. Likewise, there were 247,366 suspensions in the same time period which was an increase of 35% from the previous year. Although the number of permanent exclusions was slightly lower than the final pre-pandemic autumn term when there were 3,200 permanent exclusions, the number of suspensions is significantly higher (39%) than the pre-pandemic figure. Figures published in November 2024 by Gov.uk show that for the full year 2022/23:

There were 787,000 suspensions in the 2022/23 academic year
This is an increase from the previous year, when 578,300 suspensions occurred, and the highest recorded annual number of suspensions. This is the equivalent of 933 suspensions per 10,000 pupils.

There were 9,400 permanent exclusions in the 2022/23 academic year
This is an increase from 6,500 in 2021/22 and the highest recorded annual number of permanent exclusions. This is the equivalent of 11 permanent exclusions for every 10,000 pupils.

The most common reason for suspensions and permanent exclusions was persistent disruptive behaviour

Persistent disruptive behaviour accounted for 48% of all reasons given for suspension and for 39% of reasons for permanent exclusions. This is in line with previous years where this reason was the most commonly recorded (Gov.uk, 2024).

As well as the rise in suspensions there has been a dramatic rise in the number of pupils assessed as requiring an Education, Health and Care Plan (EHCP). The number of initial requests for an EHCP has risen from 64,555 in 2017 to 138,242 in 2023. The percentage of all children with an EHCP in England has risen from 2.8% in 2015/16 to 4.8% in 2022/23 (Gov.uk, 2024).

The proliferation of schools adopting authoritarian and oppressive practices raises questions about the underlying reasons and efficacy of such methods. Are these approaches truly in the best interests of all children, and what evidence supports their effectiveness? What is driving this increase? Are schools panicking as they appear to be "losing control" and then resorting to ever-increasing draconian measures in a vague attempt to redress the balance? Relying solely on the outcome of Ofsted inspections for validation may be too narrow an approach; do we need to start to consider a different approach?

It is necessary to look back before we can move forwards. How did we end up in this current educational landscape? Which political decisions were made, and how have they influenced school policy? We must then contrast these developments with insights from neuroscience research, challenging conventional beliefs to shed light on alternative perspectives regarding methodologies.

A Victorian Education – "Spare the rod and spoil the child"

It wasn't until 1880 that the Education Act made attending school compulsory, and this was only for children between five and ten years of age. It took another 11 years for an Act to be passed ensuring education was free for everyone. Compulsory education up to 16 years of age wasn't to become policy until 1972.

The Victorian schools faced a few problems, some of which you might just find familiar:

- Teacher recruitment (compulsory schooling was new; there just weren't enough teachers)
- Class size (these could consist of 70 to 80 children in poor inner-city areas)
- Discipline (see below)
- Attendance (low-income families relied on the extra income their children received from going to work)

The Victorians did have a clear approach as far as discipline was concerned. This was a societal view and was not limited to schools. They believed children should be "seen and not heard." Children were expected to behave at all times (at home and in school) and "to speak only when spoken to."

> Strong discipline was seen as an important part of bringing up a child. Influenced by religious beliefs, "Whoever spares the rod hates his son, but he who loves him is diligent to discipline him" … strict discipline in school would prepare them for a life in the factory, field, or home.
>
> (British Schools Museum, 2019)

The Victorian approach to discipline was described in the 1899 book *Pupil Teachers' and Scholarship School Management*, written by Arthur T. Flux for teachers:

Discipline must be natural
Discipline must be regular
Discipline must be just
Discipline must be unobtrusive
Discipline must be firm

> Punishments included lines, after school detentions, corporal punishment and expulsion. Shaming tactics, such as the dunce's hat, were also used with the intention of embarrassing children to try harder.
>
> (British Schools Museum, 2019)

Humiliation and Shame

Many primary schools still use traffic-light behaviour systems on the walls … The names are there, for all to see, on the classroom wall.

We need to be aware of how humiliation can be inadvertently used to drive a reward or sanction process ... charts and public exposure that attempts to change behaviour have long-lasting negative impacts on children, particularly those who have a history of trauma or anxiety.

(Whitaker, 2021)

I think the key point here is that in 144 years, whilst context has changed, the key issues schools face have not changed, and we seem to be no clearer on how to address these issues. I hope that this book will start to offer a way forward.

The Warnock Report

The work of the Warnock Committee started in 1974 and was set up by Margaret Thatcher, the then Education Secretary. The purpose of the review was to "review the educational provision ... for children and young people handicapped by disabilities of body and mind" (Warnock, 1978).

The findings of the committee included:

- Using the term "children with learning difficulties" instead of pupils being referred to as "educationally sub-normal"
- Heads of ordinary schools should delegate responsibility for special needs to a designated specialist teacher
- Special classes and units should wherever possible be attached to and function as part of ordinary schools
- All courses of initial teacher training should include a special element

There were 220 recommendations in all.

The report formed the basis of the 1981 Education Act, which urged "the inclusion of special needs children in mainstream classes" and introduced the system of "statementing" children to give them entitlement to special education support.

The report considered the particular needs of children with different disabilities, such as visual disabilities, hearing disabilities, physical disabilities, children with epilepsy, and children with emotional and behavioural disorders. Interestingly, children in the last category were described as "maladjusted." The report did acknowledge that the "disorders spring from many causes, including difficult home circumstances, adverse temperamental characteristics and brain dysfunction."

The report concluded that further research was needed in a number of areas, including:

- The study of those factors in school, particularly in secondary schools, which can reduce the occurrence of learning and behavioural difficulties.
- Forms of school organisation for maladjusted children in ordinary schools and elsewhere.

I wonder how much that research has informed the trend towards more authoritarian schools because all the way back in the 1980s there was a recognition that "wherever possible children with learning difficulties should function as part of ordinary schools." This seems paradoxical as many schools now feel they can't meet need.

When I came into teaching, the findings of the Warnock Report 1984 were clear. It stated that:

> Segregated special schools should be for those with the most complex and multiple disabilities which were long-term, and that mainstream schools should develop to meet the needs of all other children.

Somewhere, it seems we have forgotten or lost or maybe even purposefully ignored this message.

> Mainstream schools should develop to meet the needs of all other children.

It could be argued that the pressure on mainstream schools is unprecedented. This has been accentuated by the recent SEN "crisis." More children are receiving Education Health and Support Plans (EHCPs), and it seems that more plans are naming specialist provision. The problem is that there simply aren't enough places in special schools for all the children being named. Possibly because of the increasing pressure the schools find themselves under, they have become over-reliant on EHCPs as a tool to effectively exclude children. Some mainstream schools state they "cannot meet need," and although this is the case for the students with the most complex needs, this is not the case for all students. Some schools appear unable or unwilling to develop the skills to meet the needs of the children with mental health needs. This may be partly but not wholly down to funding.

Specialist provision, at present, is a one-way door. In my experience, some children who have specialist provision named initially, with the right support and provision, would be able to return to mainstream and access the curriculum successfully later down the line. However, examples of this are few and far between. There is a disconnect.

In the time since the publication of the Warnock Report, there has been significant development in our understanding of how the brain works and how this impacts learning, particularly but not exclusively for those children who experience difficulties. In the early 2000s, the government published its research around the Social and Emotional Aspects of Learning (SEAL) project.

Social and Emotional Aspects of Learning (SEAL)

At the school level, SEAL is characterised by the following principles:

- SEAL implementation is underpinned by clear planning focused on improving standards, behaviour and attendance.
- Building a school ethos that provides a climate and conditions to promote social and emotional skills.
- All children are provided with planned opportunities to develop and enhance social and emotional skills.
- Adults are provided with opportunities to enhance their own social and emotional skills.
- Staff recognise the significance of social and emotional skills to effective learning and to the well-being of pupils.
- Pupils who would benefit from additional support have access to small group work.
- There is a strong commitment to involving pupils in all aspects of school life.
- There is a strong commitment to working positively with parents and carers.
- The school engages well with other schools, the local community, wider services and local agencies.

(Humphrey et al., 2010)

There is not much in that list with which I would disagree, and the training materials that were produced certainly warrant being dusted off and updated. However, ultimately SEAL, first introduced to schools in 2003, failed. The report concluded, "in terms of impact, our analysis of pupil-level outcome data indicated that SEAL (as implemented by schools in our sample) failed to impact significantly upon pupils' social and emotional skills, general mental health difficulties, pro-social behaviour or behaviour problems."

Any impact that SEAL could have had was lost in the sheer amount of research and publications circulated to schools through the National Strategies. Schools were flooded with initiatives on "Behaviour and Attendance," "Gifted and Talented," "Narrowing the Gap," "Subject Leadership," and "Assessment," as well as "the National Numeracy and Literacy Strategies" and individual subject documents.

The research report on the impact of SEAL rightly identified "staff will and skill" as crucial for successful implementation. However, this was its "Achilles heel," and it remains a significant risk factor for all change management. Any approach to behaviour improvement needs unwavering, school-wide support. It must be endorsed, understood, and driven from the very top of the hierarchy, starting with CEOs and headteachers before being cascaded throughout the whole school community. All staff (and this includes lunchtime supervisors, caretakers, and cleaners) must be equipped with the knowledge behind Relational Inclusion, particularly the neuroscience that underpins its effectiveness.

The training for SEAL was delivered by local authority behaviour consultants, many of whom lacked the inside knowledge of each school's unique culture or the influence to transform it. One consultant I encountered left our school abruptly as they became overwhelmed by how our students behaved. I could almost see the slowly sinking recognition that there was no way they could manage or control these children.

Another attempted a demonstration lesson but gave up within minutes. Transferring a theoretical idea, written in the safety of an office several miles away from any children, into a form of working practice is something of a challenge, especially for someone who hasn't been in their own classroom for several years. Training effectiveness hinges on passionate experts who fully grasp and advocate the principles they wish to share.

Every Child Matters

No analysis of "how we got here" could ignore the role of "Every Child Matters" (HM Government, 2003). A government initiative launched in 2003 partly in response to the death of Victoria Climbié, this was a major turning point in re-evaluating how we worked with children. Its five outcomes were being healthy, staying safe, enjoying and achieving, making a positive contribution, and economic well-being. Each of these had further aims. Staying healthy included physical health, mental and emotional health, sexual health, healthy lifestyles, and choosing not to take illegal drugs.

Reminiscent of the "schools that don't shout" headline, isn't "Every Child Matters" an interesting phrase for a national school initiative? Is the implication that before this point, every child didn't matter? Or that "some" somehow mattered more than "others"? Equally, is this not the most sensible fundamental driver for education and any service that involves children?

Around this time, I interviewed unsuccessfully for my first Deputy Headship. I was required to complete a presentation on "How Every Child Matters" and "How I would demonstrate this." I was allowed ten minutes. The irony of the allotted time is only apparent now.

On reflection, I was being asked, as a school leader, to demonstrate why every child matters. Is this not a sad reflection on the state of play of schools' national strategies in the early 2000s? There is a rule of thumb in teaching, and it's a good one. It simply asks you to view any given situation in terms of how you would feel if it were your own child. Is it fair to assume that up until this point in time, some children didn't matter? I am ashamed to ask that question.

Looking back on my career, I can remember many of the discussions, meetings, training sessions, and leadership meetings devoted to "Every Child Matters." What I can't remember is how this fundamentally changed the lives of those pupils who struggled with past trauma and poor mental health, or any training packages written to address this.

School Inspections

One way to influence school culture and practice is through an accountability framework. All schools want to do the best for the communities they serve and often work in very difficult situations, with a significant lack of support and resources, to do the best for all pupils. After sustained criticism of school standards, the Office for Standards in Education (Ofsted) was created in 1992, with the first inspection taking place in 1993.

Originally, schools were given six weeks' notice, and inspections would last for four to five days. Schools would be graded on a seven-point scale from "excellent" (1) to "very poor" (7). The handbook included evaluation criteria with descriptions of what "good" (3) and "satisfactory" (4) would mean in all aspects of school life to be judged. Ministers had previously criticised (Her Majesty's Inspectors) HMI reports for lack of clarity, and all reports were now to follow a single framework with the same main headings:

- Basic information about the school and its pupils
- The inspection's main findings and key issues for action
- Standards of achievement (progress) and quality of learning
- Efficiency of the school
- Pupils' personal development, behaviour and attendance
- Subjects of the curriculum
- The factors contributing to the findings, including teaching quality, assessment, curriculum quality, special educational needs, equality of opportunity, management and resources, pupil welfare and parental links.

(Elliott, 2012)

Educational standards were judged purely on the results achieved by pupils, and these were displayed in tables at the front of the reports, which sometimes stretched to 50 pages, along with data on attendance, exclusions, pupil destinations, and financial information. Typical comments about behaviour included: "The school is an orderly community. Behaviour is generally satisfactory though there are isolated boisterous incidents which are dealt with promptly and effectively" or "In some cases there is weak classroom management."

In 2011, Ofsted added a new judgement which covered the "Behaviour and safety of pupils." Here they would consider the "pupils' attitudes to learning and conduct in lessons and around the school" and "how well teachers manage the behaviour and expectations of pupils to ensure that all pupils have an equal and fair chance to thrive and learn in an atmosphere of respect and dignity" (Ofsted, 2012).

An "outstanding" grade would be awarded if children were "highly adept at managing their own behaviour in the classroom and social situations." It was possible to get a good grade if "pupils, including those with identified behavioural difficulties, respond very well to the school's strategies for managing and improving behaviour."

The message is clear: Schools trying to support children who struggle with behaviour regulation cannot be awarded an "Outstanding" grade under the Ofsted framework.

In 2019, Sean Harford, then National Director of Education, stated in his blog published by Gov.uk that:

> Some will be disappointed to see that, so far, schools with more pupils from deprived backgrounds are still less likely to be judged good than those from more affluent backgrounds under the EIF, just as they were under the last framework. There's currently no clear difference in the proportion of schools judged outstanding in deprived areas, but the overall numbers are small.
>
> (Harford, 2019)

Amanda Spielman, former Chief Inspector of Ofsted, admitted that the old framework made it "harder to get a good or outstanding grade if your test scores are low" as a result of a "challenging or deprived intake" (Allen-Kinross, 2019). Where schools chose to address the root causes of poor behaviour through a trauma-informed approach, it seems at best a school could only be good. To be outstanding, it appears a school would have to be able to "fix" children of their trauma. Imagine. Why should any school go into an inspection with a limit on how well they can do because of the nature of their intake?

The frameworks are constantly evolving and being updated, and there are some positive changes in the framework that was issued in April 2024. There is an expectation that schools

> create a calm and orderly environment in the school and the classroom, have clear routines and expectations for the behaviour of pupils across all aspects of school life, not just in the classroom and have clear and effective behaviour and attendance policies with clearly defined consequences.
>
> (Ofsted, 2024)

Although the sentiments of the changes to the framework published in April 2024 seem to be a step in the right direction, there still seems to be a subjective element of how this is translated into judgements about schools.

The Ofsted view of exclusions is that they are a "vital measure for headteachers to use. However, inspectors will recognise when schools are doing all that they can to support pupils at risk of exclusion, including through tenacious attempts to engage local support services." This at best seems paradoxical and at worst seems a vague attempt to recognise an issue without truly addressing it.

In order to be graded as outstanding, the following criterion has to be met:

> Pupils behave consistently well, demonstrating high levels of self-control and consistently positive attitudes to their education. If pupils struggle with this, the school takes intelligent, fair and highly effective action to support them to succeed in their education.

Perhaps this framework does offer a beacon of hope for the future. It could incentivise schools to include children with behaviour regulation challenges, rather than resorting to exclusion or suspension or labelling them with special needs that "can't be met" in mainstream settings. However, it also offers a potential "get out of jail free card." It is vague enough to allow for unvalidated subjectivity, which could enable a claim that schools *can't meet need*. This is further endorsed by the line which states:

> In order to be good schools must not tolerate low-level disruption and pupils' behaviour does not disrupt lessons or the day-to-day life of the school.

It seems that the emotive "must not tolerate" leaves no room for interpretation. If schools choose to follow this literally, then surely, they must exclude. This leaves little room or desire to understand the developing brain, trauma, and the root cause of the problem. The true success of this framework will depend on inspectors' interpretation and how effectively it's implemented in practice.

Should we be more curious about the impact of Ofsted? The following advice, which was offered to parents, must surely be heeded:

> We find there are almost no differences in future academic, behavioural, school leadership and parental satisfaction outcomes between schools rated as good, requiring improvement and inadequate in the inspection data available to parents at the point of school selection. That is, parents who choose a "good" secondary school for their child will not leave with appreciably better outcomes than a parent who selects an "inadequate" school. The one exception to this is an Outstanding judgment, which does predict future academic outcomes – though only if the inspection was conducted within the last

five years. We thus advise parents that – besides choices involving Outstanding schools – Ofsted judgments are of limited use to them in selecting a school.

(Bokhovea et al., 2023)

Reflection

I started by asking how we got here. And now it seems, to some extent, maybe we haven't got anywhere. Is it possible that 144 years ago, the Victorians struggled with many of the same issues we face today?

If we are to move forwards, if we are going to provide a truly 21st-century education, there are some key lines of enquiry (and I don't use that phrase accidentally) we must follow and address:

1. Why are more and more children struggling to attend our schools?
2. Why are some children struggling with consistent emotional dysregulation when they are in school?

> Dysregulation is when a student is in crisis and is struggling to manage their emotions. Emotional dysregulation is a poor ability to manage emotional responses or keep them within an acceptable range of typical emotional reactions such as sadness, anger, irritability, and frustration.
>
> By using the term dysregulation as opposed to "kicking off" or "tantruming" or "ballooning" we recognise that this is a nervous system response as opposed to a chosen behaviour.

3. Why is there a problem with recruiting and retaining staff?

The puzzle before us is multi-faceted. In this chapter, I have discussed a host of initiatives and strategies which seem to have been able to identify key issues and then successfully skirt around them without addressing or having a real impact on the key lines of enquiry as identified above.

What we seem to avoid is bringing a strategy around understanding behaviour to the very front of the queue – as opposed to either demanding certain behaviours or making excuses for them. It also seems that we are not very good at letting go of the past. Phrases like "must not tolerate" fit comfortably with the Victorian age. Surely our language and understanding have moved on since then. From an educational perspective, we seem obsessed with placing more and more layers over a cracked and increasingly fractured and fragmented system. Isn't it time for change? Isn't it time for a new perspective? This book explores how Relational Inclusion can be used to support a new approach.

References

Allen-Kinross, P. (2019, December 16). Schools with deprived pupils 'still less likely to be judged good', admits ofsted. *Schools Week.* https://schoolsweek.co.uk/schools-with-deprived-pupils-still-less-likely-to-be-judged-good-admits-ofsted/

Atwood, M. (1985). *The handmaid's tale.* McClelland and Stewart.

British Schools Museum. (2019, January). *Carrot and stick: Reward and punishment exhibition book.* https://britishschoolsmuseum.org.uk/media/1677/carrot-and-stick-exhibition-booklet-lo-res.pdf

Bokhove, C. J., Jerrim, J. J. & Sims, S. (2023, February 27). How useful are ofsted inspection judgements for informing secondary school choice? *Journal of School Choice, 17*(1), 35–61, https://doi.org/10.1080/15582159.2023.2169813

Desautels, L. L. (2020). *Connections over compliance.* Wyatt-MacKenzie Publishing.

Elliott, D. A. (2012). *Twenty years inspecting English schools – ofsted 1992–2012.* Research and Information on State Education.

Gov.uk. (2024, June 20). *Special educational needs in England.* Explore Education Statistics. https://explore-education-statistics.service.gov.uk/find-statistics/special-educational-needs-in-england

Gov.uk. (2024, July 18). *Suspensions and permanent exclusions in England.* Explore Education Statistics. https://explore-education-statistics.service.gov.uk/find-statistics/suspensions-and-permanent-exclusions-in-england

Harford, S. (2019, December 16). *Our latest statistics: A first look at the EIF.* Ofsted: Schools and Further Education & Skills (FES). https://educationinspection.blog.gov.uk/2019/12/16/our-latest-statistics-a-first-look-at-the-eif/

HM Government. (2003). *Every child matters.* The Stationary Office.

Humphrey, N., Lendrum, A. & Wigelsworth, M. (2010). *Social and emotional aspects of learning (SEAL) programme in secondary schools: National evaluation.* Department for Education.

Jessup, S. (2024, February 22). *The school where teachers never shout at children.* BBC News. https://www.bbc.co.uk/news/articles/c0d7409zyzno

Ofsted. (2012, April 3). *The framework for school inspection from January 2012: Guidance and grade descriptors for inspecting schools in England under section 5 of the education act 2005 from January 2012.* Digital Education Resource Archive (DERA). https://dera.ioe.ac.uk/id/eprint/14077/

Ofsted. (2024). *School inspection handbook.* Retrieved April 5, 2024, from https://www.gov.uk/government/publications/school-inspection-handbook-eif/school-inspection-handbook-for-september-2023#evaluating-behaviour-and-attitudes

Warnock, M. H. (1978). *Report of the committee of enquiry into the education of handicapped children and young people.* Her Majesty's Stationery Office.

Whitaker, D. (2021). *The kindness principle: Making relational behaviour management work in schools.* Independent Thinking Press.

Chapter 2

Guiding Principles

Schools aren't always easy places to navigate either for staff or for the children and young people. I guess this applies to all places of work. Sometimes we get so wrapped up in our own difficulties that we don't even notice the impact, both positive and negative, we are having on those around us. One thing is for certain, there are times when we all have our up and our downs. As Charles Glassman says, "Kindness begins with the understanding that we all struggle." And if we apply this to all that we do, as often as possible, we make the world a better place for everyone. This chapter will explore the guiding principles which underpin *Relational Inclusion*.

***

I have heard a lot of people talk about a trauma-informed, or trauma-responsive, or trauma-aware approach. But when I wanted to bring it to my school, there wasn't really an approach available. There were lots of ideas but nothing concrete. There were pockets of really good practice, but I couldn't find a cohesive approach which incorporated all the latest research and thinking, was flexible enough to adapt to changes in research, and was bespoke enough to work across multiple school settings.

I decided to develop my own approach and identified five guiding principles which underpin Relational Inclusion:

> **1. We believe that if a child could do better, they would**
>
> Many children and young people don't know why they behave the way they do. As a result of early negative experiences, their autonomic* nervous system is convinced that adults cannot be

DOI: 10.4324/9781003532866-3

> trusted, and all environments contain hidden threats. We understand that we all play a role in supporting a child to do better.
>
> *involuntary or unconscious

There is still a perception among some professionals who work with children and young people that a child's behaviour is mostly down to choice. I can think of many situations in my own life where I have not behaved "well," such as shouting abuse at a fellow motorist who has done something not to my liking, or where I have not felt very safe, and I have later regretted my actions and words. I can honestly say, even though I have been appalled at my reactions, I never once thought about what I was going to do and then chose to behave badly. These reactions are autonomic; it is my nervous system trying to protect me. I am not excusing bad behaviour and choices; I am simply saying that certain circumstances lead me to react in certain ways. This may well lead me to reflect on my behaviour and change it next time, but it doesn't prevent my initial response. This comes from an adult with many years of life experience. I am not someone who generally flies off the handle. I imagine that every adult reading this will understand the feeling. Why do we think that with children it should be different? These are the people who are learning about life and relationships.

Not too many years ago I worked with a school who openly and honestly declared that they had to "defeat defiance" as though it was a war that could be won with clear consequences and strict discipline. I am not proud to say that I played a part in the creation of that system.

I have had many interesting conversations with teachers about their response to "defiance." In one school, all behaviours had been graded on a scale of 1 to 4, with 4 being the worst and likely to lead to exclusion. Initially, defiance was placed at level 4, along with racism and violence towards another. But then some teachers recorded incidents as level 4 when a pupil had refused to remove their coat, even though the list of behaviours was so extensive that "failing to remove a coat in class" was in the list at level 2. Clearly this is an abuse of the system and should not have happened. It illustrates two things: Firstly, that a tariff behaviour system is open to interpretation and this lack of consistency is problematic for teachers and pupils alike. Secondly it illustrates that there will always be teachers who are part of the "sit down and shut up brigade." They believe that children should do as they're told instantly and if they don't, they should be punished. This desire for a pound of flesh is not dissimilar to the Victorian approach to behaviour. They seem to think that there isn't much that a pupil could do that is worse than defying an instruction from a teacher. Do we want children to obey unquestioningly because they are scared of being punished, or do we want them to make the right choices for the right reasons because it is the right thing to do?

Instead of relying on immediate compliance, teaching children self-regulation is a long-term investment. This approach builds the neural networks that empower them to manage their emotions and behaviour from within. Fear-based external controls may work in the short-term, but they lack lasting effectiveness.

This idea of defiance is not uncommon. The implication is clear. Children come to school with a fixed mindset and are determined to do everything they can to wind up their teachers, consciously break rules, and challenge authority.

This is a belief system based on blame. When the children can't be controlled, their parents are brought in because if it's not the child's fault it must be down to parenting. After all, this chosen behaviour must be someone's fault, surely.

In the last four years I have worked more closely supporting secondary and primary school leaders. And it is not uncommon to receive a phone call where a headteacher calmly explains how a child has "chosen" to throw a chair or assault a member of staff or smash up a classroom.

Sometimes the child being discussed is four or five years old. This doesn't seem to change the narrative in the heat of the moment. This is why our first guiding principle is so important. It may seem controversial. It might challenge your current system of belief. But if we start from a place where we believe everyone, especially children, is doing the best they can, then we can begin to reframe our approach and attitude towards discipline.

The most common reason given for permanent exclusion in the United Kingdom is "persistent disruptive behaviour." Again, the implication is that children are choosing to be persistently disruptive to the point that they don't deserve a place in a mainstream school. Imagine if we renamed this "consistent emotional dysregulation." Now we are understanding that a child is unable to consistently manage their emotions. If this is the case, then their behaviour is being driven by their nervous system. They are hypervigilant and in survival mode. Their brain has triggered fight or flight. "What is adaptive for children living in chaotic, violent, trauma-permeated environments becomes maladaptive in other environments – especially school" (Perry & Winfrey, 2021).

The children are doing the best they can in the circumstances in which they find themselves. They are certainly not "choosing" to be defiant. As Annette Breaux (a motivational speaker) says, "Nine times out of ten the story behind misbehaviour won't make you angry it'll break your heart."

This book delves into strategies aimed at supporting children who face challenges in managing their emotions, assisting them in recognising and responding to their feelings in a more constructive way. It also investigates how schools can, and should, adapt to cater to the needs of these children. Whilst there are no quick fixes and no miraculous remedies to avert emotional breakdowns in struggling children, the collective effort of schools in accommodating and supporting these individuals can go a long way in creating more inclusive learning environments. Traditional behavioural strategies such as shouting, threatening, and whole-class punishments had adverse effects on all children, not just those demonstrating challenging behaviour. Well-behaved children can be frightened by angry teachers, even though the aggression is not aimed at them. Equally the threat of whole-class punishments is unjust. These strategies may have impact in the short term but are ineffective over time, leading to further negative emotional responses.

- A discipline model over-activates the fear system.
- When a pupil's fear system is activated they are more likely to move into the lower part of their brain
- They have no capacity for reflection or "making good choices"
- They only have the capacity for reactivity – to defend and attack
- Initially this may give compliance but this can quickly move our traumatised pupils into difficult states like fear and terror.

(Bombèr, 2020)

2. Relationships, Relationships, Relationships

By relationships we mean:

- The *relationship* from the student's perspective
- The *relationship* from the staff's perspective

> - "The priority given to *relationship* formation and maintenance from school leadership" (Riley, 2011)
> - The relationship we have with ourselves and our own well-being
>
> We understand that positive staff–student relationships have been shown to contribute to students' attendance, academic grades, psychological engagement, and reduced disruptive behaviours. We know that supportive staff–student relationships can also help in overcoming family education disadvantage.
>
> We know we must recognise *blocked care** and our risk of slipping from our social engagement system.
>
> *when it becomes difficult to remain open and engaged

Once I became accustomed to the fact that in schools, behaviour systems and policies don't actually work, that the idea of power and control is actually a series of fictitious mind-games and kidology, I realised that schools and their staff thrive and survive (or fail) on relationships. Although there are probably more, the second of my guiding principles identifies four key relationships.

The first key relationship is how schools consider their interaction from the students' perspective. As adults we make a lot of presumptions about how people feel but how do we really know how children and young people feel in our schools? This is not so much about capturing student voice in a survey; it is more about having a culture and ethos where children feel safe, feel seen, feel heard, and are supported. Are we asking our children the right questions? When I was talking to my staff about the importance of our students feeling safe, one of my teaching assistants replied that she tells her students they are safe every lesson. This is the subtle difference – we can't tell someone they feel safe, they must feel it for themselves, and this can be a very slow process. It starts with recognising that we must "live, not laminate," the constant creation of a climate and culture which recognise and facilitate the importance of empathy.

> Duncan Craig OBE, CEO of We Are Survivors and childhood abuse survivor, explains:

> When I look back now (of course with hindsight) I can see that there were possible changes in my behaviour and mood that I think, if asked the right questions, would have elicited a different response and maybe give teachers and adults in positions of trust an insight into what was happening behind closed doors. For example, I can remember being asked by my Form Tutor, "All ok?" and I remember saying, "Yes." because I was expected to say yes; but I wonder if I had been asked, away from everyone else in class, something like, "You look a bit like your mind is elsewhere Duncan, is there anything that's confusing you at the moment in class or outside?" I think I might have felt like I was being invited to talk, especially as the "OK" isn't used and as it feels like an observation was being made. Does that make sense? Especially as it was being asked by a teacher I kind of got on with.

The second key relationship is concerned with the relationship staff have with each other. Schools are often pressure cookers – new legislation is released, funding is cut, there is pressure on examination results, on attendance, on behaviour, and practice and process can change rapidly. This constant pressure can fracture relationships in school; staff have different beliefs and values, and the staff body can fragment into cliques. As with our students, it is important that staff feel safe, feel seen, feel heard, and are supported. It is important that schools clearly identify what their expected culture is. Table 2.1 shows the cultural fit document that I use in my schools. This document is used from the application stage in our employment process.

It states: *Working in a school where you are not aligned with the culture is a miserable experience. So … we both need to have alignment if you come to work here!*

All schools have slightly different approaches and nuances. For relationships to be truly effective, it is important to support staff from the start by identifying as clearly as possible what the school's culture and ethos are. This is then further developed in the interview process and in the induction programme. We then revisit Relational Inclusion every half term through CPD.

The third relationship must come from school leadership. Relationships do occur naturally. However, to have a culture which

Table 2.1 Cultural Fit Document adapted from Putting Staff First

Cultural Fit

Working in a school where you are not aligned with the culture is a miserable experience. So … we both need to have alignment if you come to work here!

- Our Vision is for staff and students to be engaged, happy and successful.
- Our Mission is to work together to inspire, nurture and motivate everyone to fulfil their potential.
- Our Core Values are respect, trust, confidence and courage.
- We believe that staff come first.
- We believe that we all have a professional obligation to improve as teachers, instructors and teaching assistants. We are a learning community.
- We believe that every child deserves a Champion.
- We believe in a culture of the possible, where we can all make progress beyond what anyone, including ourselves, could have imagined.
- We believe in the TEAM and we support each other continuously.
- We believe in talking first.
- We believe that truly great teaching is that which improves students' progress.
- We believe an evidence-informed approach to teaching and learning helps us identify what works best in the classroom.
- We believe that hard work is the key to success for staff and students.
- We believe that you cannot just wish for staff and students to be better – you have to create the conditions for them to grow.
- We believe basic literacy and numeracy are essential to students making good progress.
- We welcome diverse ideas to solve problems and are solution focused.
- We value generosity of spirit.
- We acknowledge that we all make mistakes.

- In this school we integrate therapeutic and Relationally Inclusive interventions into our everyday practice.
- From research we are aware that any disruption within the early years from pregnancy onwards can impact minds and bodies in three key areas: Affect (emotion) regulation, attachment and executive function.
- From research we understand that the toxic stress involved in ACEs impacts the nervous system of human beings.
- From research we know that over-compensatory, rich, relational interventions can bring about recovery so that children and young people can function well at home, school and out in their communities.
- We view ourselves as an important part of any pupil's recovery journey. We believe in recovery in community.
- We will not discriminate how we relate to the pupils in our care as we believe each pupil is worthy of our time, energy and patience. However, we will differentiate, according to need.
- We will have compassion for those who are dysregulated, are hurting and/or grieving for whatever reason.

Source: Tomsett & Uttley, 2020

recognises the importance of relationships, this cannot be left to chance. All too often a leadership's perception of its relationship with its staff and students differs to the perceptions of the staff and of the students. A relationship process must be consciously crafted by the leadership team; this has to be constantly revisited and remain high profile, and it has to be part of the golden thread which binds a school community together.

The final relationship, and possibly the relationship we give least thought and time to, is the relationship we have with ourselves. In every school I have ever worked in, as we draw closer to the end of a term, staff become increasingly red faced and short tempered. Temperatures rise and yet for the most part, we repeat this cycle without understanding why this might happen. We are only human and wonderfully human.

It is important to commit time and training to understanding how our brains and bodies work. We must support our staff body in recognising the impact Adverse Childhood Experiences (ACEs) can have on their well-being. We must help staff understand their own attachment history and how this might affect their emotional responses. We must help staff understand and recognise their window of tolerance and how it fluctuates. We must support staff in understanding and recognising vicarious trauma and how this can impact on our daily practice. This must always be carried out from a place of safety. We must have a culture that recognises all of these experiences as a normal part of existence. This can only be achieved through a regular CPD programme.

ACEs

Adversity leads to toxic stress which affects how we learn, how we parent, how we react at home and at work, what we create in our communities, and **more learning difficulties and behavioural problems in school-aged children.**

Adverse Childhood Experiences	Adverse Community Environments
Physical abuse	Poverty
Emotional abuse	Violence
Sexual abuse	Community disruption
Physical neglect	Poor housing quality and affordability
Emotional neglect	Discrimination
Divorce, separation, death	Lack of opportunity, economic mobility, and social capital
Mental illness	
Domestic abuse	
Substance abuse	
Incarceration	
Frequently moving home/school	

Why ACEs are so important

Four or more ACEs can lead to an increased chance of:

- Chronic depression
- Attempted suicide
- Alcoholism
- Intravenous drug abuse

Four or more ACEs can mean a person is more likely to display high-risk behaviours such as:

- Smoking
- Obesity

- Unintended pregnancy
- Multiple sexual partners
- STDs

Four or more ACEs can mean an individual is 50 percent more likely to suffer the following long-term effects:

- Lung disease
- Heart disease
- Liver disease
- Cancer

We also use a daily check-in in our schools. The process and rationale are outlined below.

Why We Check in

- A daily check-in builds self-awareness and emotional intelligence
- We work with children suffering a great deal of toxic stress
- We therefore are at risk of vicarious trauma and blocked trust on a daily basis
- We need to work as a team so that we remain within our window of tolerance, and we need to recognise in ourselves and each other when this is not the case so that we can support one another and co- and self-regulate ourselves

Similarly, our students need us to be operating in our optimal window of tolerance as they need our help to co- and self-regulate. As we know:

We will either co-regulate
or we will co-dysregulate.
They will catch our calm
or they will catch our anxiety. (Young, n.d.)
Therefore, we meet to check in every morning.

During check-in we:

- **Share a thought for the day or a question which we discuss:**
  The purpose of this is to help us regulate; to remind us that we are a professional body and a team; to move from our personal world to our professional mindset.

- Share how we are feeling or where we are in our own window of tolerance:

1 Very disconnected
2 Disconnected
3 Slightly disconnected
4 Very dysregulated
5 Dysregulated
6 Slightly dysregulated
7 Narrow window of tolerance
8 Calm window of tolerance
9 Optimal window of tolerance

The purpose of this is to recognise where we are at the beginning of the day; to remember we are at risk of vicarious trauma and blocked trust; to help us co- and self-regulate; and to identify and support any potential dysregulation or disconnection among staff so that we are best placed to help and support not only our colleagues but also our dysregulated students.
- **Complete a mindfulness activity, such as a breathing exercise**

Why a check-in is important:

In our morning check-in a member of staff looked particularly ashen. When I asked how she was feeling, she explained that she "wasn't great." She went on to explain that her journey to school had been a little traumatic. Another driver had undertaken her on the motorway. As they had passed her, she had stuck two fingers up at them. In response they pulled in front of her and slammed on their breaks. She was slightly embarrassed to admit she had stuck up two fingers, but we had created a safe place where she could talk openly without fear of being blamed. This meant that we could put steps in place to co-regulate her until her nervous system had calmed.

By having a check-in, we can start to create a safe place for our staff. Not only does this support staff but it is also a pre-emptive as opposed to a reactive strategy. If I had not picked up how my member of staff was feeling in the example above, she may have gone home sick, or she may have behaved out of character with her class. Her dysregulation may have triggered dysregulation in a student or another member of staff.

Individuals co-regulate one another's physiology which means that the quality of a person's relationships and social interactions shapes their development and health, both of the body and the brain (Immordino-Yang et al., 2018).

Window of Tolerance

The window of tolerance is a term coined by Dr Dan Siegel (1999). Our window of tolerance is the space we sit in when we are balanced and calm. To some extent it is our coping space, our mood organ.

Some days you wake up and nothing can shake you; you take everything in your stride and manage problems without them becoming stressful – when you operate in this space you have a wide window of tolerance.

On other days everything appears to go wrong. Your children have been up all night, you stood in cat sick, your little boy has just sneezed on your clean shirt, your daughter has tipped her breakfast all over herself, you get to the car and have a flat tyre.

On days like these, the next thing that happens is going to make you snap – you have a narrow window of tolerance.

The window of tolerance is not fixed; I like to think of it as elastic. It stretches and shrinks; it changes from minute to minute and hour to hour. When it's narrow, your responses are less reasonable; you are emotionally tense. When it's wide you are much more balanced, and your responses are much more thoughtful.

I will discuss later useful exercises around the window of tolerance.

Guiding Principles 45

> **3. We accept all emotions but not all behaviours**
>
> We see all behaviours as an opportunity to learn. We believe in the unconditional acceptance of the emotional experience that lies behind behaviour, whilst communicating that the behaviour is indeed unacceptable for the child's life as it gets in the way of healthy relationship development or learning.
>
> We believe that discipline is based on the needs of the young person, not our adult wants.
>
> We develop strategies aimed to work with a student's biology instead of against it.
>
> We understand that co-regulation must occur before self-regulation can be learned.
>
> We know that a child must "feel safe" and not be told they are safe.

For some reason the United Kingdom seems relatively stuck in the way we respond to emotions. We seem trapped in time, still wedded to the old-fashioned, Victorian "stiff upper lip" approach. As a result, we tend to respond to emotional outbursts with a pat on the back, a comment like "there, there" or "chin up son," and an expectation to get on with things.

We seem very uncomfortable with the idea that "it is okay not to be okay," despite the fact that this is a perfectly normal part of life and we all experience it. Many children are unable to explain how they are feeling, and this can result in them "behaving their feelings." The consequences of this can be self-harm, poor emotional regulation, mental health problems, depression, social anxiety, etc.

Being able to put your feelings into words is called "affect labelling." Research shows that if we work with children to help them label their emotions, this can calm the nervous system, reduce distress, and decrease amygdala activity. The amygdala is the part of the brain that is most associated with fear, emotions, and motivation.

Many schools use the *Zones of Regulation* (Kuypers, 2011) to help young people identify different emotions and this is important. However, it seems to be that again we fall into a very British trap. We label emotions as either good or bad. It is bad to angry or sad; it is good to be happy or excited. Once again, I must stress, it is so important to highlight that all emotions are okay. There are no "bad" or "negative" emotions. It is essential to work with young people so that they understand how they feel, so they can recognise where on their body they feel particular emotions. It is also important to highlight that though the feelings are okay, it is certainly not okay to punch or to kick or to act out their feelings. This is where we must work on co- and self-regulation which we will discuss later.

Some of the greatest misunderstandings in this kind of practice are that it makes excuses for poor behaviour; that this approach means children cannot be given consequences; that there are no rules and no boundaries. It is very important that this myth is dispelled for this is not the case at all. This approach is based on holding boundaries firmly and fairly with understanding and with empathy. See Table 2.2 for further misconceptions and the supporting explanations.

> Boundaries are the walls that keep the house up. Trauma Informed Practice is firm on the behaviour, but gentle on the child.
> (Trauma Informed Schools UK, n.d.)

Relational Inclusion means that all emotions are okay. It also means that, if the emotions are accompanied with difficult behaviours such as swearing, or kicking, or spitting, or damaging property, these behaviours must be addressed.

During a recent learning walk, I witnessed a student storm out of a classroom, slamming the door. Unable to intervene directly, I observed as she kicked and knocked on the door of a nearby classroom.

The teacher, her form tutor, emerged calmly and asked, "What can I do for you, lovely?" The student, visibly upset and agitated, explained that her previous teacher wouldn't believe she'd already completed the assigned work and asked if she could have her work to take back to the teacher.

The form tutor, demonstrating respect, retrieved the work and returned with a book. The student, now composed, thanked her and quietly returned to her original class.

This encounter highlights the importance of setting expectations for behaviour alongside empathy. Whilst calming the student and validating her feelings were crucial, a missed opportunity existed. The form tutor should have gently reminded her that kicking doors is unacceptable, even when frustrated. It was a perfect chance for the student, who clearly respected her teacher, to learn a valuable lesson within a supportive environment.

Table 2.2 Some Misconceptions about a Relational Inclusion Approach

Misconception	Reality
You can't exclude or give consequences.	Children will thrive from firm boundaries and consistency (even if the child displays dysregulation).
Children (and some staff) will think this approach means children can get away with things and that excuses are being made for poor behaviour.	Boundaries are the walls that keep the house up. Relational Inclusion is firm on the behaviour, but gentle on the child. Shouting, threatening, and shaming overstimulate the fear response. You may get a quick win but the child is then only capable of a reactive response, as they are working from the lower part of the brain.
If they do something wrong, this approach means we can't address it.	We address this by reflecting on the behaviour, not shaming the child; maybe just a tweaking of consistent language is what's required. Consequences should actually be **learning opportunities**. "If a child can't read, we teach, if a child can't behave, we..." Children need to be shown a positive process of rupture and repair and a clear message that it's okay to get something wrong.
If we move away from a rigid tariff system behaviour will go through the roof.	Wondering with curiosity and empathy to co-regulate has more long-term impact than a tariff behaviour system where we are following procedures (i.e. phone calls, recording incidents) but not meeting the needs of the child. A Relationally Inclusive system created by you, for your school, is reflective of your culture, demographic, and character. One size doesn't fit all. Every system takes time and effort. Remove the shame; develop the child's confidence. This approach takes courage and vulnerability. It might take us out of our comfort zone but ultimately it better meets the needs of our children and young people.
We need a clear system such as "red cards" or "C1-C3" so that children know where they stand.	From a child's perspective, these systems make the children feel that they are not good enough or are shamed. It makes them ask, what's the point? It can make them think that their teacher doesn't like them (the child personalises the teacher's use of the system).

Understanding how we talk to young people and what we hope to achieve from our interactions is crucial. But how do we talk to children who are emotionally dysregulated? This is easier said than done, and we also must be able to manage our own emotional regulation. That being said, there are a few key strategies that we can employ. Table 2.3 identifies three behaviours we tend to turn to.

Table 2.3 Three behaviours we turn to when addressing dysregulation

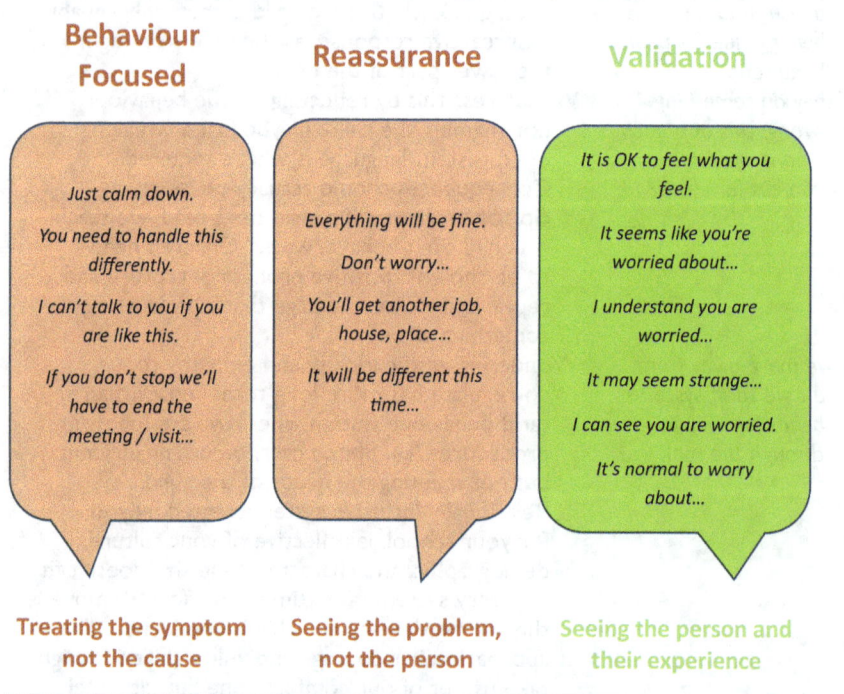

4. We identify and address the cause not the symptoms

Beneath every behaviour there is a feeling. And beneath each feeling is a need. And when we meet that need rather than focusing on the behaviour, we begin to deal with the cause not the symptoms (Ashleigh Warner). We understand that complicated behaviour deserves a more complex response which involves a "state-dependent" intervention rather than a one-size-fits-all response.

It is so important to have a full understanding of what children and young people experience outside of school and before they arrive at school. As in the poem below, for some children, just getting to school is a massive achievement and we must not underestimate the impact this has on their nervous system and their ability to focus and to learn new information.

Often these children arrive at school and, instead of seeing a friendly face and being praised for their self-management skills under really challenging circumstances, they are reprimanded before they even get into their classrooms.

Cause I Ain't Got a Pencil

By Joshua T Dickerson
I woke myself up
Because we ain't got an alarm clock
Dug in the dirty clothes basket,
Cause ain't nobody washed my uniform
Brushed my hair and teeth in the dark,
Cause the lights ain't on
Even got my baby sister ready,
Cause my mama wasn't home.
Got us both to school on time,
To eat us a good breakfast.
Then when I got to class
The teacher fussed
Cause I ain't got a pencil

I visited a primary school three years ago to begin a Relational Inclusion pilot. These visits always begin with a tour of the school. As we talked in one of the playground spaces, one child stood out. He never made eye-contact; in fact he never looked at us. He never came close enough to draw attention to himself but wherever we went, he moved his game so that we were always in his line of sight.

When we returned to the headteacher's office, she began to describe a little boy who she was really struggling with. She explained that every morning he arrived at school and then would dysregulate. Sometimes this would last for ten minutes, sometimes it would last until lunchtime.

Often, he became very violent and would throw things and break things. Inevitably he would end up hiding under a table.

This is a story which I have heard multiple versions of. Sadly, it usually results with the headteacher saying something like, "We have exhausted all possibilities. We have several hundred children, and they are all scared. My staff are getting hurt. Parents are complaining. I can't risk the safety of my staff and my students. I'm afraid I have no choice but to permanently exclude."

Fortunately, this headteacher had a very different view and had invited me in to see if together we could find an alternative approach. I described the boy who had kept us near to his circle of play and not surprisingly, of all the children in the school, it was the same boy. I asked her to tell me what she knew about this child's background. Again, she provided a fairly familiar background.

The boy was one of seven siblings, two of which were always in care. Rarely the same two. His mum dropped him off every morning and he seemed regulated when he was with her. The dysregulation began as soon as she tried to leave.

I stopped the conversation. I am not a therapist or a counsellor. Sometimes you just need a different pair of eyes viewing the same situation through a different lens. I suggested that maybe the dysregulated behaviour began because of his uncertainty of what might happen when his mother left. Who would be at home at the end of the day? Whose "turn" would it be to be taken into care? Then I predicted that maybe he had circled us that morning because I was unfamiliar – maybe it was his turn, and I had come to take him away.

If that was you and you were worried that if you let your mum go, you might not see her again, but if you clung on, just maybe you might be able to prevent things happening to either you or your siblings, might your behaviour be a little unsettled? Even as an adult? What if then you were forced apart from your mum and saw her leaving the building? Would you calmly follow a teacher's instruction and walk happily to your next lesson? Would you be able to sit down quietly and settle into your learning? I know for certain that I would fight like hell to reach out to my mum, even now, and she's 77!

We discussed this further, and I asked the headteacher whether, if she knew this would happen every day, they had done anything differently each day. In schools we often are so busy that we take a reactive approach rather than a proactive approach. She then said that they hadn't, they did the same thing every day, but then she remembered one day that had been different.

On this day, by chance, in her assembly she had carried out a mindfulness breathing activity. She has an exercise where she asks the children to "smell the flowers and blow out the candles." Having participated in this assembly, the little boy didn't dysregulate that morning. We had our light bulb moment.

This is why it is so important to take the time to try and work out what is really going on, to find the cause of the child's issues as opposed to addressing the symptoms they display. What is the lived experience of our children? What are they trying to tell us without words? The solution isn't simple. It isn't a quick fix. The boy still dysregulates; however, the length of his dysregulation has much reduced. Some days he doesn't dysregulate at all. But the school, the leaders, the teachers, and the support staff all have an understanding of where this behaviour is coming from and how to manage it. The boy hasn't been permanently excluded and no-one feels unsafe.

In the words of the headteacher, "The little boy was in year 1 when you first heard of him. He's now in year 3. I don't want to jinx it, but it's been 18 months since he had a bad morning. Transitions are still tricky, but we pre-empt this with provisions. His home life is still chaotic but in school he is engaged and calm."

5. We foster a culture of compassion and repair

Compassion to accept the individual experience: Why people are suffering and what has happened to them.

Compassion of understanding: Every function is an adaptation, and everyone is doing the best they can with the resources they have inside them and around them.

Compassion of possibility in the here and now: Every interaction is an opportunity for repair, reattunement, and growth for a positive vision of the future and self.

Compassion for the importance of voice, choice, and empowerment: We give voice and offer choice within our relationships with children, families, and staff and are inclusive in the process of transformation.

We repeat what we do not repair.
(attributed to multiple people in the therapeutic field)

When I began this journey and introduced the need for "repair" into my schools I was often met with challenge. Some staff said to me, "It's okay, I don't need a restorative meeting." And this highlights a key misunderstanding. I have purposely avoided the term "restorative conversations" in my more recent leadership roles and practices. This is mainly because the restorative systems I had access to didn't quite achieve what I wanted to achieve. When I completed my diploma with Trauma Informed Schools UK, they used the word "repair" and I found this much more fitting.

What I wanted my staff to understand was that when things go wrong, when behaviour is challenging, when mistakes are made, as they inevitably are in all schools, it is our job to model how to put things right, how to "repair" the situation and move forwards, and this is can be a challenge.

Firstly, if we, as staff, are dysregulated we can sometimes take behaviours and comments personally; we are after all, only human. Unfortunately, sometimes this leads us down a "self-gratification" pathway. We want "justice," we want "our pound of flesh." The first lesson here from Relational Inclusion is that we need to ground ourselves. We need to remember that this is not personal. We need to remember that the young person is trying to communicate something to us, and we are not in the right place to receive this – our window of tolerance is too narrow.

I find the poster below useful to share and discuss with my teams.

Five Things to Remember When Working with Challenging Behaviours

1. Don't take it personally.
   It's not about you.
2. The behaviours are challenging.
   The child is not.
3. De-escalate first.
   Problem solve later.
4. Sometimes we might not see it, but
   There's always a reason.
5. Have empathy.
   Just imagine what the child is going through.

(pathway2success, n.d.)

Secondly it is important to remember the multiple worlds our children and young people live in outside of school. They have rules at home, they have rules on the street with their friends, they have the rules of their society and the rules of their culture. They then have the rules of their primary school which may not be the same as the rules of their secondary school. If they have moved schools several times as well for a variety of reasons, then there are a whole host of slightly contradictory school rules to learn and understand. As school leaders there is an expectation that they follow our rules blindly, that they adopt them through osmosis. When do we take the time to discuss and share and check understanding?

Our children and young people live in multiple worlds with multiple rules, of which they have little control and sometimes little understanding. We don't want to reinforce shame and negative patterns of behaviour and thinking. It is vital that we teach our children that it is okay to get things wrong and that we all make mistakes. When we make mistakes there can be logical or natural consequences and this is okay. This is how we repair and move forward. When an adult takes the time to work this through with a child consistently, then children feel safe to make mistakes, to ask for help, to try and put things right, and this also helps them avoid having "to repeat what they do not repair."

Table 2.4 Guiding Principles – Summary

1. We believe that if a child could do better, they would
Many children and young people don't know why they behave the way they do. As a result of early negative experiences, their autonomic* nervous system is convinced that adults cannot be trusted and all environments contain hidden threats. We understand that we all play a role in supporting a child to do better. *involuntary or unconscious
2. Relationships, Relationships, Relationships
By relationships we mean: • *Relationships* from the student's perspective • *Relationships* from the staff's perspective • The priority given to *relationship* formation and maintenance from school leadership (Riley, 2011) • The *relationship* we have with ourselves and our own well-being.

(Continued)

Table 2.4 (Continued)

We understand that positive staff–student relationships have been shown to contribute to students' attendance, academic grades, psychological engagement, and reduced disruptive behaviours. We know that supportive staff–student relationships can also help in overcoming family education disadvantage. We know we must recognise *blocked care** and the risk of slipping from our social engagement system. *when it becomes difficult to remain open and engaged
3. We accept all emotions but not all behaviours
We see all behaviours as an opportunity to learn. We believe in the unconditional acceptance of the emotional experience that lies behind behaviour, whilst communicating that some behaviours are indeed unacceptable for the child's life as they get in the way of healthy relationship development or learning. We believe that discipline is based on the needs of the young person, not our adult wants. We develop strategies aimed to work with a student's biology instead of against it. We understand that co-regulation must occur before self-regulation can be learned. We know that a child must "feel safe" and not be told they are safe.
4. We identify and address the cause not the symptoms
Beneath every behaviour there is a feeling. And beneath each feeling is a need. And when we meet that need rather than focusing on the behaviour, we begin to deal with the cause not the symptoms (Ashleigh Warner). We understand that complicated behaviour deserves a more complex response which involves a "state-dependent" intervention rather than a one-size-fits-all response.
5. We foster a culture of compassion and repair
• Compassion to accept the individual experience: Why people are suffering and what has happened to them. • Compassion of understanding: Every function is an adaptation, and everyone is doing the best they can with the resources they have inside them and around them. • Compassion of possibility in the here and now: Every interaction is an opportunity for repair, reattunement, and growth for a positive vision of the future and self. • Compassion for the importance of voice, choice, and empowerment: We give voice and offer choice within our relationships with children, families, and staff and are inclusive in the process of transformation.

Reflection

Look at the summary of the guiding principles in Table 2.4 and consider the following questions. This is an exercise that can be completed by an individual, by a senior leadership team, and by the whole staff body.

- Which of the guiding principles do we already follow and are embedded into our everyday practice?
- Which of the guiding principles do we agree with but haven't become part of the culture and ethos of our schools? What are our next steps?
- Which of the guiding principles do we find the most difficult to accept?
- Why might this be and what do we need to do to address this?

References

Bombèr, L. M. (2020). *Know me to teach me: Differentiated discipline for those recovering from adverse childhood experiences.* Worth Publishing.

Immordino-Yang, M. H., Darling-Hammond, L., & Krone, C. (2018). *The brain basis for integrated social, emotional, and academic development: How emotions and social relationships drive learning.* Aspen Institute. https://www.aspeninstitute.org/wp-content/uploads/2018/09/Aspen_research_FINAL_web.pdf

Kuypers, L. (2011). *The zones of regulation: A curriculum designed to foster self-regulation and emotional control.* Social Thinking Publishing.

Pathway2Success. (n.d.).

Perry, B. D., & Winfrey, O. (2021). *What happened to you? Conversations on trauma, resilience, and healing.* Bluebird.

Riley, P. (2011). *Attachment theory and the teacher–student relationship.* Routledge.

Siegel, D. J. (1999). *The developing mind.* Guilford Publications.

Tomsett, J., & Uttley, J. (2020). *Putting staff first.* John Catt.

Trauma Informed Schools UK. (n.d.). *Practitioner training: Trauma and mental health informed schools and communities: Delegate handbook.* https://www.traumainformedschools.co.uk/

Young, K. (n.d.). *Big feelings: The training ground for self-regulation.* Hey Sigmund. https://www.heysigmund.com/big-feelings-self-regulation/

Chapter 3

Relationships, Relationships, Relationships

I was listening to the radio on my way into work and Mel Robbins (a motivational speaker) was talking about "high fiving yourself in the mirror." She said, "As ridiculous as it sounds, if you do it, it's impossible not to smile, and that one act can change your mood for your day." When I got to work, I couldn't help but try it, even though the idea made me feel a bit silly. She was right though. There I was, beaming back at myself. As humans we are emotional animals. As Maya Angelou says, "I've learned that people will forget what you said, people will forget what you did, but people will never forget how you made them feel." This chapter will explore the importance of relationships and the impact they have on our behaviour.

***

Why Would Anyone Want to Be a Teacher?

The more I think about it, the more I realise that teaching is quite a strange career choice. I often wonder if anyone ever really considered the implausibility of classroom dynamics? Compulsory education means that from the age of 4 to 16, children are taught in classes of around 30. Usually there is one teacher and sometimes there is a teaching assistant. Just take a minute to consider that. In what other situation is 1 person expected to manage and control another 30 in a relatively small space, every hour for 5 hours a day? It wouldn't be too bad if children were little machines who did exactly what they were told as soon as the instruction was issued. Fortunately, children aren't machines. They bring a cacophony of unpredictability to every situation. It's the teacher's job to keep the beat over what can very quickly become a very chaotic orchestra. It's a wonder that any of us survive.

They say "everyone remembers their favourite teacher" and I think this is true. I think it is also the case that everyone remembers their worst teacher. What is it that makes a good (or a bad) teacher? I don't mean this from a performance management perspective or an Ofsted perspective. I mean it through a child's eyes. I asked my own children this question and, without hesitation, they replied: "A good teacher is funny, kind and respectful." Who can argue with the honesty of an eight- and a six-year-old?

From a child's perspective, or at least my memory as a child, teachers weren't really human. They didn't really exist outside of school. I thought teachers lived in school. They certainly didn't have a life outside of school, which made it a bit weird when you saw them at the supermarket or in town, wearing "normal" clothes, sometimes even with their own families. That just wasn't right at all.

Good teachers make learning interesting. And somehow, somewhere, you know they really care. In fact, the really great teachers make everyone in the class feel special. As though you are the only one that matters.

I can remember marking the first homework I'd ever set. I wondered what the hell had happened; did my teaching exist in some kind of parallel universe? Not one of the children had written anything remotely to do with the lesson I'd taught. After a little reflection and self-evaluation (and I think as teachers we often (over) scrutinise the lessons we have taught) I realised that in this particular lesson, to demonstrate a key piece of learning, I'd told them a loosely linked anecdote. In my mind I had beautifully illustrated a real-life example of whatever the subject was I was trying to teach.

The "problem" was that the anecdote was the thing the class had remembered. This is what had stuck in their minds. They'd totally missed the "important" point of my lesson and the crucial aspects of the curriculum. Or had they? They had responded to my enthusiasm; the zest and the life I had related through my story had sparked their interest. Because this was real. This was genuine. They had experienced my passion and my honesty, and something had resonated.

At several points in my career, I can remember saying to various classes who were probably bored and disengaged, "I'm not here to entertain you, I'm here to teach you." And I meant this sincerely.

However, there is nothing like a group of teenagers sitting yawning in front of you to give you a reality check. The truth is, that when our interest is captured, when we are entertained, when we are gripped, that is when we learn. I think the best teachers are also entertainers. I don't mean that they are stand-up comics or perform a tap-dance, at least not literally. I mean that they make learning entertaining. Not all teachers do this in the same way but when teachers entertain, when it "works," everyone in the room can "feel" it. The learning and the engagement are tangible, you can quite literally "taste" it.

No matter how engaging and captivating the subject may be, if a child does not feel secure or valued in the classroom and is not respected by the teacher, the environment for learning becomes compromised, leading to potential behavioural challenges. I have witnessed numerous instances where staff grapple with apparent behavioural issues. However, these situations usually arise from a lack of understanding from both parties. If staff were able to "helicopter" themselves into a position where they could look down on the escalating situation, they would see that it was in fact a combination of their own behaviour and that of the child's.

Most staff will experience this multiple times throughout their careers. The helicopter analogy is a useful training tool when helping staff and teams reflect on incidents that have occurred and seem to have escalated rapidly, apparently out of nowhere. As a deputy headteacher, I recall an encounter with a particular child who, despite my positive relationships with most students, seemed to single me out, whenever our paths crossed. It felt like he was goading me and targeting his disruptive behaviour directly at me.

I distinctly remember being on duty in the canteen. Like some kind of heat-seeking missile, this student would seek me out and then push every button he could to wind me up, demonstrating as much disruptive behaviour as he could muster. This behaviour not only stirred feelings of anxiety within me but also influenced my decision-making process, as I found myself taking his actions personally without even thinking about trying to understand what the root cause might be. It is very hard to detach ourselves from our emotions when we feel under threat.

This situation culminated in a surprising and swift resolution. I had to carry out a scheduled Spanish lesson observation and to my horror, "you know who" was sitting in the class. Adding to the tension, the only available seat for me was next to him. My knowledge of him thus far had been limited to his disruptive behaviour, seemingly targeted at me. However, this situation provided a change of context. I was amazed to discover that he had exceptional ability in Spanish. He exhibited respect towards the teacher, absolute attentiveness, and eagerness to participate, and all of this was reflected in his meticulously maintained exercise book, a tangible display of his pride in the subject.

Following the lesson, I asked the student to remain behind. I told him how proud I was of him; I said I really admired his remarkable skills and talent for Spanish. Jokingly, I even confessed my envy, as my own attempts at learning the language had been challenging. He graciously accepted my praise and left the room. The next day, as I saw him approaching from a distance, my anxiety resurfaced. However, this time, very much to my relief, the exchange was amicable; he told me about that day's Spanish lesson and offered me helpful phrases for my next trip to Spain. From that point on, our interactions were marked by respect and connection rather than conflict.

This experience taught me that his initial behaviour was not about me "personally" but was likely triggered by associations from past experiences where he felt uncomfortable or unsafe. Once I took the initiative to connect with him, he responded positively, transforming into a friendly and cooperative student. Our newfound connection dispelled my anxiety, enabling a harmonious relationship to flourish.

This is further supported and therefore less surprising when we consider some of the neuroscience that is taking place in the background. When we feel safe, calm, connected, and engaged our brain reward system releases "happy" hormones: Dopamine, oxytocin, endorphins, and serotonin (see Table 3.1). These are our body's natural opiates, and they make us feel good. When we feel seen and heard and valued, the polyvagal theory suggests that we are in a place of social engagement. In simple terms this is our "sweet spot"; it means we are in the perfect place to learn, and it means that our executive functioning is fully operational. Executive functioning is the skills we learn to help us get things done (see Table 3.2).

Table 3.1 Hormones Released by the Brain Reward System

Happy Hormones

Dopamine – the reward chemical
Triggered by:

- Completing a task
- Achieving a goal
- Food
- Self-care

Oxytocin – the love hormone
Triggered by:

- Socialising
- Physical touch
- Animal petting
- Helping others

Endorphins – the painkiller
Triggered by:

- Exercising
- Music
- Laughter

Serotonin – the mood stabilizers
Triggered by:

- Sun
- Nature
- Meditation and mindfulness

Table 3.2 The Eight Executive Functions

The Eight Executive Functions

Impulse (or Self-) Control
The ability to stop and think before acting

Self-Monitoring
The ability to evaluate your own behaviour

Emotional Control
The ability to manage your emotions and control your behaviour

Flexible Thinking
The ability to adapt to changing conditions and adjust plans and strategies

Task Initiation
The ability to start and finish tasks and avoid procrastination

Organisation
The ability to keep track of tasks both mentally and physically

Working Memory
The ability to use the information held in your memory to complete a task

Planning and Time Management
The ability to create steps to achieve a goal

(ADDvantages Learning Center, n.d.)

Executive Function

> Executive functions [are] a set of cognitive processes that are essential for the cognitive control of human behaviours.
>
> (Atkins, n.d.)

> Executive function and self-regulation skills provide critical supports for learning and development. These skills help us remember the information we need to complete a task, filter distractions, resist inappropriate or non-productive impulses, and sustain attention during a particular activity. We use them to set goals and plan ways to meet them, assess our progress along the way, and adjust the plan if necessary, while managing frustration so we don't act on it. Although we aren't born with executive function skills, we are born with the potential to develop them. The process is a slow one that begins in infancy, continues into early adulthood, and is shaped by our experiences. Children build their skills through engagement in meaningful social interactions and enjoyable activities that draw on self-regulatory skills at increasingly demanding levels.
> (Center on the Developing Child, n.d.)

For all the inspirational teachers, there are those who don't seem to quite get relationships right. For children, these are the teachers who can be perceived as being *mean*. According to my eight-year-old: "They are strict, they shout, and they are kinder to other teachers than they are to children." I can remember dreading going into year two because of the teacher. She was small and scary. She was strict (although I didn't know the word then) and I was so scared of getting into trouble with her that I couldn't concentrate on my classwork. My hands sweated so much in fear of getting something wrong that I had to keep a towel in my tray. When she was cross her fury filled the whole room. It wasn't only me who felt this way. My friend began bed-wetting again, triggered by being in her class.

To this day, I can't understand why anyone would want a five-year-old to be so terrified of their teacher. I can't imagine or allow myself to believe that this was intentional. Did she really become a teacher to scare very small children? I don't know if she will ever read this book, but I would love to ask her whether she was self-aware enough to know the fear she struck into the children in front of her, whether it was intentional or not.

One of the schools I worked in specialised in supporting children with social, emotional, and mental health difficulties. A new member of staff had been appointed, who on paper had the right educational training and background, but in practice lacked experience in handling the challenging behaviours presented by our students. They faced significant difficulties even though they were surrounded by a training package and supportive colleagues who had a wealth of experience and understanding of "our" children's needs.

Over time, they encountered several challenges from different children, and they consistently struggled to establish meaningful relationships. The first incident saw them being wrongly accused of something and this reminded them of a negative experience in a previous school. On this occasion we decided to move the challenging pupil to another class. However, the issues persisted, culminating in another difficult situation with a different student. This resulted in the staff member expressing their frustration through emotionally charged emails and demanding immediate action to be taken regarding the child's behaviour. It's important to place these events within the specific context of the school; there was no option of giving him an easy class. Equally we could not keep removing pupils from his lessons.

The child at the centre of these challenges came from a background marred by severe trauma, including prolonged exposure to domestic violence and a distressing episode where he was kidnapped by his father, leading to his removal from the family home. Such experiences undeniably influence a child's behaviour and reactions to various situations.

Awareness of a child's traumatic past should fundamentally inform and shape the approach taken when interacting with them. Unfortunately, the staff member in question focused solely on the child's misbehaviour, failing to consider the underlying causes. This lack of empathy and understanding was further compounded by the staff member's physical presence. He was a large, imposing figure with a deep, loud voice, traits that could unintentionally trigger fear or anxiety in a child with such a traumatic history.

The member of staff also failed to consider his own positioning and body language when engaging with the child. He placed himself between the child and the door. Such behaviour is likely to provoke a defensive or adverse reaction from a child in "fight or flight." Similarly, towering over a child whilst they remained seated, physically dominating a space, is counterproductive to building trust or a positive rapport.

In essence, the disparity between the child's need for understanding and the staff member's approach demonstrated a missed opportunity to foster a positive, supportive relationship. By not adapting his behaviour or considering the impact of his physical presence, he inadvertently perpetuated a cycle of misunderstanding and conflict between an adult and a child. This illustrates the vital importance of empathy and adaptability in educational environments, particularly those serving children with complex backgrounds and emotional needs. This example serves to emphasise how a deeper insight into both our own behaviour and that of others can play a crucial role in effectively managing challenging situations.

Again, an understanding of neuroscience is important. What happens to our brains when we are scared? As humans were once hunter gatherers, our survival instinct is strong. Our bodies *err* on the side of caution as a protective measure. When we sense fear, the following happens:

1. Our amygdala sounds the alarm (there is more about our friend the amygdala later)
2. Our brain triggers fight or flight and produces adrenaline
3. Adrenaline makes our heartbeat faster and stronger
4. Our airways open up so that we can take in more oxygen
5. Our blood pressure rises, sending blood to our skeletal muscles so that we can run and jump and do all that is necessary to escape
6. Our body converts fat into sugar to give us the energy we need to protect ourselves
7. Adrenaline and noradrenaline act as a stimulant. This helps us think more clearly and work out our quickest path to safety
8. Adrenaline and noradrenaline also create euphoria. I like to think of this as our Incredible Hulk syndrome. It gives us the belief and therefore strength to think that we can conquer the world
9. At this point our heart is pumping, our muscles are primed, and we are ready to fight
10. To enable this our fear centre temporarily shuts down the thinking part of our brain (pre-frontal cortex) – we need to defy the odds, and our rational brain would be busy telling us that our survival strategy was ridiculous

This process happens to all of us. It happens when a driver cuts us up on the motorway. It happens when we hear a loud and unexpected noise. It can happen in an argument or because of a perceived sense of conflict. It happens with children and adults equally.

It also means that this impacts negatively on our ability to learn. When fight or flight is triggered, we are no longer in a state of social engagement and consequently our executive function is compromised; this is known as "executive disfunction." We become hypervigilant. Look again at points 7 and 8 above. We switch to survival mode and the way our brain and body work changes. Table 3.3 demonstrates how this impacts us.

Even more concerning is that fight or flight isn't only triggered because of (un)intentionally "mean" teachers. If a child is living in a "state of trauma," sadly this is how they feel and how their body responds for a large majority of their lives. This alone should help us reflect on the way we sometimes use the term "chosen behaviour" as far as children are concerned. (Trauma is discussed in more detail in the next chapter.)

In the same way that we have "happy" hormones, we also have stress hormones (see Table 3.4). In the short term these hormones raise our heart rate and increase our blood pressure and blood sugar which gives us an "energy boost," improving our physical performance. They stop us feeling hungry, suppress our immune system, and keep us alert. These hormones are necessary for survival; they are designed to protect us. However, over activation can lead to chronic stress which contributes to physical and mental health issues.

With all this going on inside our bodies and minds and children and young people's bodies and minds, you might begin to wonder, why did we ever become teachers?

I think this is a really important question and I don't think enough time is given to supporting "new" teachers in exploring why they have

Table 3.3 How Our Brain Reacts in Survival Mode

This Happens in Our Body:	This Happens in Our Mind:
Our ears tune into a high or low frequency	We become pre-occupied
Our breathing becomes fast or shallow	We become hypervigilant. Think meerkat!
Our heart beats fast	We constantly assess potential threat
We can't find our words	We feel aggravated
Our stomach feels churned up	We feel on edge
We get very hot or very cold	We have a sense of feeling trapped or cornered
We can't keep still	We can only think in terms of the next second or minute

(Bombèr, 2020)

Table 3.4 The Stress Hormones

The Three "Stress" Hormones
We have three primary stress hormones: Cortisol, adrenaline, and noradrenaline.

Adrenaline prepares the body for a "fight" or "flight" response in the face of stress, fear, or excitement.

Cortisol helps the body maintain balance during stressful situations by adjusting our glucose, immune response, and blood pressure.

Noradrenaline is also involved in our "fight" or "flight." This helps us regulate our attention; it helps our learning, memory, and mood.

(Jaiswal, 2024)

come into the profession and what they hope to achieve. Are they aware of their journey back into the classroom and how this alone may impact upon the young people in front of them? After all, for the vast majority of teachers, their only experience of school before becoming a teacher is as a pupil.

They say teaching is a vocation but in reality, there are many reasons why we come into teaching. Some teachers have a real passion for their subject. They studied it at A level and degree; maybe they have a master's and a doctorate. They want to share this wonderful knowledge and learning with the children in front of them.

Some teachers watched *Dead Poets' Society* and wanted to inspire or influence a new generation. They want to challenge children into thinking outside of the box, to change a piece of the world a classroom at a time. They see so many children waiting to soak up knowledge, be inspired, and take on the world.

Some teachers found schools to be the only place they were accepted and seen and heard. They were made to feel important in and by school and they want to pass that feeling onto other children.

Sadly, I imagine there are also a few teachers who come into teaching for power and control. And some who come for the paycheck.

Anthony's Story

For me, I never wanted to be a teacher. My mum was a primary school teacher, so I had the unusual experience of growing up on both "sides" of the classroom. I guess the rules in schools were a bit different back then. There were lots of times when I went to school with my mum and spent the day in her classroom. I'd work with different groups of children, listening to them read, helping them with their sums. At play time they transformed me into some kind of human climbing frame and would play fight and climb me. As I got older, I was allowed to take groups outside and teach them PE.

As I said, I never wanted to be a teacher. I didn't like the system; it seemed neither fair nor equitable. My mum said that this wasn't really an excuse. She said that if I didn't like something I could either complain about it or I could get inside it and change it.

At 19 years old, having spent a year doing bits and pieces and not really managing to find my place in the world, I signed up for my PGCE and decided that I was going to change the world. It's taken me 27 years to admit that. I didn't want to punish children. I didn't want to frighten them. I wanted to work with them and alongside them, to help them see the world and the opportunities that were available to them. I think that this is the way we can make the world a better place.

The truth is I had always really enjoyed working with children. It came easily and naturally for me. I think, given the right chances and openings, children are full of life and energy. When they make mistakes – well they're just children, it's their job to make mistakes. How else do they learn? I had less tolerance for grown-ups. With children I had much more patience and time. I always found it quite easy to help them bounce back up and find a new or different way of doing things. I could always find a way of capturing their interest or excitement. I believe that the world should always be a new and exciting place for children.

When I stepped into my first classroom, I don't remember feeling scared or nervous at all. It felt like I was exactly where I should be. I seemed to be able to find the balance between making learning enjoyable whilst maintaining rules and high expectations (and unfortunately a bit of shouting).

What I now know is that the children felt safe in my classroom. I had clear rules and expectations. There was always time for discussion. We talked through things as they arose and most importantly, I liked the children in my classes and because they sensed this, they liked me.

Alan's Story

I don't remember consciously deciding to become a teacher; it kind of happened organically. As a gay child and then a young adult in the

1970s, my pathway wasn't exactly straightforward, and I had a real desire to break free from the confines of my upbringing. For me, university was a refuge; it gave me the opportunity to discover myself and find my place in the world amidst the social challenges and the limited representation of diverse identities which existed at the time. The course I chose to study wasn't so pivotal for me in those days.

Due to my dad's job, we often relocated during my formative years. In an era when the internet hadn't yet been invented, this made it a real struggle for me to make meaningful connections and relationships, and so the school environments stood out as beacons of hope. Although it took me until my 40s to openly embrace my true self, the significance of education in shaping my identity and aspirations was undeniable. Comprehensive schools fostered my enthusiasm for the arts and humanities, although sometimes my enthusiasm had to top up the occasional lack of natural ability. My exposure to a broad range of subjects opened my world and instilled in me the belief that learning was a gateway to empowerment.

Once I'd finished university, I found myself at a bit of a crossroads. As I was the first in my family to complete higher education, I recognised that schooling had a transformative power in opening doors to possibilities which I had previously thought were beyond my reach. I was comforted by the positive impact of teachers who had inspired and guided me along the way. It was this realisation which pushed me to pursue teaching as a career. I was driven by a deep-seated desire to uplift others and foster social change. I was motivated by the opportunity to repay the opportunities I had been fortunate enough to receive, to a new generation of students, particularly those hailing from working-class backgrounds. I wanted to contribute to the creation of a more equitable society where education could be the catalyst for progress and personal growth.

Securing my first job as a maths teacher in Greater Manchester posed something of a problem. I was hindered by my physics background as schools seemed to want maths graduates. How times have changed! Schools today would fight for a maths teacher with a physics background. The landscape is so different; the demand for teachers seems more pressing than ever before. I suspect now I would get a job merely for having a pulse.

Back then, job placements often relied on Local Authorities, and with just a week remaining before the term began, I contacted the Local Authority where I had attended university. This yielded potential openings. Presented with a choice between a picturesque setting in a school described as a "nice leafy suburb with good families," and a less favourable option characterised as a "challenging environment with various issues," I opted for the latter out of a sense of contrariness, a decision I would come to cherish.

I joined a school in Manchester that would later be the subject of national headlines – it was labelled as "the worst school in Britain" – and I found myself thriving. Connecting with the students and families in this setting, I felt a profound sense of belonging and empathy. I formed deep-rooted relationships with my first form group who became an extension of my own family. Witnessing their successes brought me immense joy, yet the struggles and barriers some of them faced served as poignant reminders of the ongoing challenges within our society.

As I reflect on my journey in education, my initial drive to uplift "broken" children and empower marginalised individuals to shape a brighter future has evolved. But the straightforward answer to why I chose to work in schools is that I simply never left.

Know Thyself

When I first moved from mainstream to special education/Alternative Provision, among the many differences (and to be fair, that's probably a whole book in itself), two things particularly stood out. The first was that as we drew near to the end of a half term, everyone's faces grew redder and redder. Tensions were high and tempers were fraught. It was as if someone had turned the temperature up to boiling point. Now I accept this also happens in mainstream but not to anywhere near the same extent.

The second thing I noticed was the "all-hands-on-deck" mentality. In mainstream this would be a positive thing but not so in these settings. If a child, or member of staff, dysregulated, the classrooms emptied, and the corridors filled. When dysregulated staff meet dysregulated students, "en masse," you get co-escalated fireworks. And they aren't pretty.

As I gradually disappeared down my trauma and attachment rabbit hole and began to develop *Relational Inclusion*, I realised that it was "us" that lay at the heart of this. If we didn't understand ourselves, our triggers, our behaviours, we didn't have a hope in hell of helping anyone else. If things were going to change, we had to shine a light on the relationship we had with ourselves.

It was necessary for every member of staff to explore and recognise why they were doing the job they did. This wasn't an easy journey, and we lost some staff along the way as they decided that this just wasn't for them. Nonetheless it was a vital first step.

The reason I have spent time in this chapter exploring *why* we enter into teaching is because those very reasons may impact on the relationship we have with ourselves and subsequently the relationship we have with our colleagues and the children and young people we teach.

If we came into teaching because of our passion for our subject and we meet a class who, for a whole host of reasons, might not share our passion, we are likely to become frustrated. If we are not aware of this, we might blame the class, we might blame individual students, we might feel targeted by individual students. We might blame ourselves or feel like we have failed. We might question whether we are actually doing the right job and need to think about a different profession. We certainly won't benefit from our "happy" hormones and may even find our stress hormones becoming over-active.

Similarly, if as children, school had been our safe place and we came into teaching to extend that sanctuary to other children, again our inner working model may be threatened or challenged. Children have a knack of finding our weak spots. If a teacher has poured their heart and soul into planning a lesson, or working with a particular group, or really supporting an individual, and that class or individual doesn't respond as the teacher hoped or expected or simply throws it back in the teacher's face, the teacher may feel rejected. This might trigger their own fight or flight responses, leading to conflict and dysregulation.

Whilst this is happening to our teachers and support assistants, similar processes are also happening for our children and young people. If we don't train our schools to consciously recognise the signs and approach such events and potential conflicts with curiosity – well, we are very quickly back to the not very pretty firework display.

We need to be in a place where our whole school community understands "happy" and "stress" hormones. If, together, we can recognise these, we can have what I like to call a "Matrix Moment" where we begin to see "through" behaviours and amend our own stress responses (self-regulate) before supporting the children to do the same (co-regulate). These "behaviours" only become "issues" if we are unprepared and they take us by surprise.

To put this into practice, I have outlined below some key strategies of how this might start to look.

Mapping Our Window of Tolerance

Schools are busy and unpredictable places, and we all experience days which don't quite start the way we would hope. Subconsciously our *internal* feelings can set our *external* mood, and this can impact on the people around us. We all know that smiles are infectious. Unfortunately, so are bad moods. We are often so caught up in our day to day lives that this goes unnoticed until something makes us snap. If we make a conscious effort to recognise our feelings, we can avoid *behaving our emotions*. In Chapter 2 I talked about the window of tolerance. A useful activity is to map a school's "window of tolerance" from multiple perspectives. This is a really simple activity which also provides a clear temperature check for your school.

The first task is for the leadership team to look at the school day through a *Relationally Inclusive* "lens." Initially, from a leadership perspective, consider when, as a team, your window of tolerance is really narrow or really broad. We can predict that stress points come at the start of the day and the end of the day, probably lunch and break, and possibly lesson changeovers. However, each school is unique, and it is worth working through this exercise together to really understand the temperature of your school at different points in the day.

Step two is to repeat the activity but this time for a week. Do particular days have different points of stress and ease? Why might this be? Is it a curriculum issue or a timetable issue? Again, we can predict that Monday mornings are likely to be an issue, possibly the last period of every day, and maybe Friday afternoons.

Step three is to repeat this activity but this time focusing on a half term. This is when I realised that the penultimate week of every half term led to increasingly red-faced staff. In my particular circumstance I believe this was as a result of vicarious trauma. Vicarious trauma is the result of working alongside others who have experienced trauma for a prolonged amount of time. Sometimes referred to as secondary trauma or compassion fatigue, it begins to impact on your own mental health. Staff with a history of trauma are more susceptible to these symptoms.

If this is the case in your school or workplace, are you aware of it? Can you pinpoint the times this is more likely to happen? And if you can then it's really important that staff understand what this is; why they may be feeling the way they do; and most importantly, if we know it's happening, what support measures we can put in place.

Step four is for the teachers and support staff (and this includes caretakers, cleaners, lunchtime supervisors, etc.) to complete steps one to three. If you are brave enough, it is worthwhile for the leadership team to try to complete this activity from a teacher's perspective. Here we are looking for alignment or points of conflict. Is the staff experience mirroring the leadership team's experience? If so, this would suggest a healthy relationship between leadership and the staff body. If not, is there something that the leadership team has missed and therefore needs to spend some time working at? There will obviously be differences due to the positions the different teams are coming from. The key is to recognise any surprises, be open to these, and address them with curiosity and a desire for improvement.

Finally, and arguably most importantly, this task should be repeated from the children and young people's perspective. Again, if you really want a true picture, the leadership team should complete this in terms of how they perceive the children and young people will respond; the teachers and support staff should do the same; and then a cohort of children and young people, possibly the student council.

Collating the findings of all these layers and then comparing and contrasting will give you a very clear picture of where you stand and where your school or workplace stress points are and more importantly help you focus on what needs to happen next. It will help shine a light on whether your perceptions of the relationships within your school or workplace are accurate or fictional.

As this exercise is also collaborative, it helps staff awareness of their own window of tolerance. Sometimes, when our window of tolerance has narrowed, we are not the best person to deal with a dysregulated student or situation, yet when the red mist descends, we are not always able to see this. We introduced a fictional "blue folder" for this eventuality. If a member of staff sees another member of staff is beginning to dysregulate, they will step in to co-regulate and ask the member of staff to go and collect the *blue folder*. This is a safe way of asking the dysregulated member of staff to step away from the situation. It is non-judgemental and creates a comfortable space where that member of staff can remove themselves safely and protect their own well-being.

Check-in for Children

When children arrive at school they are not necessarily in the ideal emotional state for learning; their executive function may be compromised. Many come to school bearing the scars from long-standing traumatic issues, whilst others might be grappling with incidents from the night before. To be in the best position to learn, it is essential for them to recognise, understand, and articulate their emotions.

In a similar fashion to the staff check-in outlined in Chapter 2, my schools have implemented a daily emotional check-in for all students. This helps them to develop their emotional literacy by providing them with a structured opportunity to reflect upon and identify their feelings. In groups, children are asked a question such as "what brings you joy?" This encourages them to discuss their emotions before going on to tell us how they are feeling that morning. In our classrooms, we support this process with a visual aid – a sheet populated with a range of emotions, each represented by a distinct emoji. This tool allows children, especially those who might initially struggle to articulate their feelings using words, to visually identify and communicate their emotions effectively. By pointing to an emoji, they can convey complex feelings in a simple and understandable way.

A daily check-in for students not only supports emotional development but also enhances the students' ability to engage with their learning environment positively and productively. Any student who is not in the right emotional state for learning can be identified during check-in and supported to regulate before moving on to face the day. Sometimes this takes longer than the time allocated for check-in and needs to be continued away from the classroom. This process is a preventative strategy to support a child's dysregulation and prevent escalation as they move through the day.

Animals and Nature

Once upon a time a Newly Qualified Teacher (NQT now known as an Early Career Teacher (ECT)) asked me if she could bring her hamster to school to keep as a pet for the Science department. I thought this was a great idea. We worked in a school which had high levels of deprivation and the more exposure we could give our children to experiences that other children took for granted, the better.

I had to run this by my boss and unfortunately the answer wasn't what I expected. I was told that animals were "something of a risk," I was told some horror stories of past experiences with school pets and was then given the following advice:

> "Why don't you suggest that the teacher gives each of the class a small plant which they could maybe name and nurture?"

I kid you not.

I didn't share that piece of advice but did have to tell the enthusiastic NQT that unfortunately we couldn't have class pets in school. The NQT left after a term for a different school. Science teachers were difficult to come by and I might be wrong, but I thought their departure wasn't helped by our apparent lack of vision to support our children.

Fast forward four or five years and during an interview I found myself in a Social, Emotional and Mental Health difficulties (SEMH) classroom which was full of reptiles. (I'm not referring to the teachers or the students.) One child had a snake across their shoulders. Another was holding a gecko. The teaching assistant enthusiastically explained how calming the reptiles were for students who were often dysregulated.

When I completed my diploma with Trauma Informed Schools UK (TISUK) they introduced me to biophilia. This is a "hypothetical human tendency to interact or be closely associated with other forms of life in nature" (*Merriam-Webster Dictionary*). Kellert et al. (1993) developed the concept of the Biophilia Hypothesis. They believe that as human beings we have an innate need to connect, not only with our own species, but with all living things. Wilson referred to our "*Siamese Connection*" without which we cannot be mentally well. If we lack connection, we can, to some degree, replace these feelings by connecting with our natural environment and the creatures within it (Trauma Informed Schools UK, n.d.).

If you were to visit my school now you would find therapy dogs, a reptile room, rabbits, rats, gerbils, guinea pigs, a hedgehog, pygmy goats, ducks, and chickens. The goats and chickens roam our outside space freely; the children collect fresh eggs daily. When we think of relationships, it is important to consider our relationship with nature. It is so important for children and young people to see that we share our living environment, not only with people but with animals. The other thing that I learned, very much to my surprise, is the calming influence an animal can have on a dysregulated child. We mustn't forget the "happy" hormones – animals can help release both oxytocin and serotonin.

Forest School

Some of us just aren't designed to sit still behind desks in neat little rows. When I have a puzzle to figure out, I need to pace; it helps me think. When I was at my first school as a teacher, we had a tiny faculty office, and I had marking to do. I tried to squeeze myself and my work into the desk but in the end resorted to sitting on the floor and spreading the work out around me. A senior teacher poked his head into the office and asked whether "I was some kind of hippy or something?"

Forest Schools are not about "mucking about in the woods." They enable some children who may struggle in a classroom environment to thrive but are not exclusively for children who "can't sit still"; they benefit everyone. Forest Schools have the same rules and boundaries as classrooms, but they are not restricted by walls and tables and chairs.

The Forest School teacher at my school has transformed a barren and wasted bit of outdoor land into the most fantastic learning environment. There are rope swings, bivouacs, shelters made from branches, and a campfire to cook on burning constantly. Children whittle, craft, and cook food. They learn social skills such as self-awareness, self-management, social awareness, relationship skills, and responsible decision making. The children are outside, whatever the weather, and they love it. Working in this environment releases endorphins, oxytocin, and serotonin.

Reflection

This chapter has explored why a deep understanding of relationships is so important if everyone in our school communities is to thrive. It has highlighted the importance of the relationship we have with ourselves and how having a better understanding of why we do what we do has so much impact on those around us.

It is important to consider:

- Have we made relationships a priority in our schools?
- Do we understand survival instinct and how stress response can affect behaviour – especially when children and young people are scared or feel threatened?
- Have we mapped out how the school operates through a window of tolerance perspective?
- Have we shaped our school environment to reflect our commitment to fostering and supporting the development of positive relationships?

I'd like to finish this chapter with a quote from Jillian Turecki (relationship coach):

Feeling safe is the single most important criteria for a relationship. It's not the only thing we need, but none of the other things matter if we don't feel safe physically, psychologically, and emotionally.

Safety is the foundation of all functional relationships.

References

ADDvantages Learning Center. (n.d.). *Executive functioning.* https://addvantageslearningcenter.com/executive-functioning/

Atkins, E. (n.d.). *Episode 1 what you need to know, to end rough sleeping.* YouTube. https://www.youtube.com/watch?v=yoy1aDqMmbk

Bombèr, L. M. (2020). *Know me to teach me: Differentiated discipline for those recovering from adverse childhood experiences.* Worth Publishing.

Center on the Developing Child. (n.d.). *Enhancing and practicing executive function skills with children from infancy to adolescence.* https://children.wi.gov/Documents/Harvard%20Parenting%20Resource.pdf

Jaiswal, A. (2024, July). *What are the 3 stress hormones and how do they impact your body?* Fitelo. https://fitelo.co/disease-management/what-are-the-3-stress-hormones/

Kellert, S. R. Wilson, E. O. & Shepard, P. (1993). *The biophilia hypothesis.* Island Press.

Lively Minds Tutoring. (n.d.). *Executive functions explained.* https://livelymindstutoring.com/2020/01/29/executive-functions-explained/

Robbins, M. (2021, 9 November). *Chris Evans Breakfast show.* Virgin Radio UK.

Trauma Informed Schools UK. (n.d.). *Practitioner training: Trauma and mental health informed schools and communities: Delegate handbook.*

Chapter 4

Don't Try to Fix Me

Many years ago, I was talking to a head of year about behaviour in school and our strategy for managing it. She said, "We've got this all wrong, you know. We wait until it's too late, until everything has gone wrong. And then we try to put a sticking plaster over it all. What we really need to do is identify this early. We need to get the support in place as soon as we are alerted to it. As opposed to letting things escalate to the point that boundaries have been crossed to a point where there is no turning back."

Some conversations you just never forget.

All of us, as school leaders, can stand at the school gates on the first day of term and identify children who are going to struggle. In fact, when my daughter started reception, my partner said a very similar thing. She could easily see the children who were going to have a tough time. Yet what do we do? We wait until a crisis happens and then we react. What if we put a strategy into place where we are proactive instead of reactive?

Desmond Tutu said, "There comes a point when we need to stop just pulling people out of the river – we need to go up stream and find out why they are falling in."

This chapter will explore why the children in our schools are not broken; why trying to "fix" them won't work; and what we need to understand to stop them *"falling in the river."*

***

A first headship is an interesting experience. Everyone is looking at you and to you, and no-one looks more critically than you look at yourself. You have to set your stall out; first impressions are everything. Those first decisions can make or break you – at least that's how it feels. So, as we often do, I started with the students. I had this idea that "if you look smart, you think smart." I think I actually convinced myself that this was true. I can remember explaining to students how the uniform helped "get them into school mode"; how it gave them a sense of identity; how it made them part of a team.

As a new head, trying to "set my standards," I banned trainers, I specified the length ties needed to be (at least three stripes), I banned unnatural hair colours and anything other than natural looking make up, I restricted piercings (one in each ear, studs only), and I locked the majority of toilets during lesson times. I controlled where and when and how the children and young people could go at any time in the day. This was a school. It was a place of learning, and I was going to manage it and enforce it carefully.

It is a common belief in schools, maybe even in society, that if we don't meticulously manage every aspect of behaviour, the school will descend into chaos. I genuinely thought that this kind of "tight" discipline was preparing our children and young people for a life beyond school. What I didn't understand was the extent of the barriers some children face outside school, making any kind of punitive discipline ineffective within school.

Interestingly, the idea of a school mode – a readiness to learn – a sense of identity, and being part of a team are the nuts and bolts of relationships and therefore education. Often schools mistakenly refer to children as not being "school ready." This indeed is an interesting concept. I would always argue it is the schools who should be ready, not the children and young people. I'm going to spend the next part of this chapter exploring what might be going on with the brain and why this must be understood and applied in all school settings before we worry about giving detentions or suspending children because of their footwear or hair colour. Are we confusing high standards and expectations with control and power?

What supports and disadvantages the ability to learn? If these "broken" children can be fixed by a dress code, a behaviour policy, silent corridors, and absolutely no coloured hair, why are the issues we are facing in schools on the increase? Why haven't strict behaviour policies solved the problem? What if the children aren't broken? What if they don't need fixing? What else might be going on – and what can we do differently?

Lessons from the Past

We talk about hindsight as being a wonderful thing, yet we have easy access to all sorts of historical documents which often we either ignore or manipulate. I think we can learn a lot if we just look back on what has gone before us and dig a little deeper. As George Santayana (1905) said, "Those who cannot remember the past are condemned to repeat it."

During the First World War, Charles Myers coined the term "shell shock" (although it could be argued that the soldiers were the first to use this name). It was believed to result from "a physical injury to the nervous system" (The National Archives, n.d.). Shell shock is important here for two reasons. The first is that:

> Inevitably, Myers was criticised by those who believed that shell shock was simply cowardice or malingering. Some thought the condition would be better addressed by military discipline.
>
> (Jones, 2012)

We have all seen the horrific black and white film clips of soldiers suffering from shell shock. It is hard, with all we know now, to imagine that anyone could have thought this was an intentional act of cowardice or simply an actual "act" put on in an attempt to avoid fighting in the war. Yet this is what some people believed. Equally to think that "better ... discipline" could address this seems a little ridiculous when we consider what life in the trenches must have been like. It is also interesting that once again the idea of "better discipline" is being used as a potential solution to mental health issues, although this was 1915.

The second reason that this is so important is that Myers "convinced the British military to take [what he said] seriously and developed approaches that still guide treatment today." His "principles of forward psychiatry" were the origins of what we now know as post-traumatic stress disorder (PTSD) (Jones, 2012).

But what has this got to do with classrooms and the behaviour of children? Let's jump forward to 1966.

The Romanian Orphans

Under Nicolae Ceaușescu, the Socialist Republic of Romania introduced a pro-natality policy. Abortion and contraception were banned. By 1977 people were taxed for being childless. Consequently, birth rates increased and many children were abandoned in orphanages. "While in these institutions, these babies were subsequently malnourished and received minimal social contact and little stimulation" (Glasper, 2020).

Although the children were fed, changed, and clothed, it seems very much that in their years of early development they weren't given love or meaningful human emotional contact.

Chugani et al. (2001) administered PET scans to a sample of children adopted from Romanian orphanages. These are scans which show areas of your body where cells are more active than others. His study of the brains of Romanian orphans showed:

> mild neurocognitive impairment, impulsivity, and attention and social deficits. Specifically, the Romanian orphans showed significantly decreased activity in the orbital frontal gyrus, parts of the pre-frontal cortex/hippocampus, the amygdala and the brain stem.
> (Chugani et al., 2001)

In simple terms, the pre-frontal cortex is a part of the brain pretty much behind your forehead. Among other things, it regulates high-order decision-making and planning. It is responsible for intelligent regulation of behaviour, thought, emotion, and empathy. Scans of the Romanian orphans' brains showed gaps in this part of the brain.

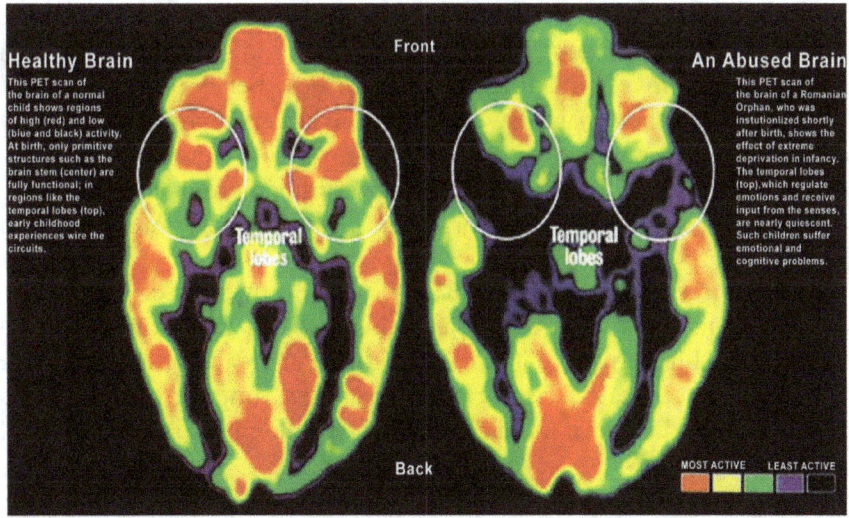

Figure 4.1 Healthy and Abused PET Scan.

When the brain scan of a soldier suffering from PTSD is compared to the scan of an abused child's brain, the images are unsurprisingly similar. In 1992, Judith Herman proposed "Complex PTSD [CPTSD] as a clinical syndrome following precipitating traumatic events ... taking place during early stages (i.e. child abuse and neglect)" (Herman, 1992).

If we put this contextually in the classroom, the pre-frontal cortex is responsible for **empathy** and **response flexibility**. The *Oxford English Dictionary* defines empathy as "the ability to understand and share the feelings of another." Response flexibility is about whatever might trigger us and our response to that trigger. The study of Romanian orphans shows us that children who are suffering from trauma and/or attachment may have gaps in the development of their brains.

As teachers, support assistants, and school leaders, when one child has dysregulated with another, we generally respond with two questions:

1. Why did you do that?
2. How do you think "they felt" when you did it?

And often the children respond with the same answer. "I don't know."

If the pre-frontal cortex has not developed or is underdeveloped, this potentially means that when children say "they don't know" in response to the two questions above, they are telling the truth. Theoretically we are asking them to explain actions they don't and can't understand, holding them to account for behaviours they can't control, and then applying a punitive punishment to rectify these behaviours. When the future choices they make haven't changed we metaphorically scratch our heads and increase the consequential behaviour tariff.

In November 2022, the British Government provided a working definition of trauma-informed practice. This definition states:

> Trauma results from an event, series of events, or set of circumstances that is experienced by an individual as harmful or life threatening. While unique to the individual, generally the experience of trauma can cause lasting adverse effects, limiting the ability to function and achieve mental, physical, social, emotional or spiritual well-being.
>
> (Office for Health Improvement and Disparities, 2022)

The Equality Act of 2010 with reference to harassment states:

> A school must not harass a pupil because of his disability – for example, a teacher shouting at the pupil because the disability means that he is constantly struggling with class-work or unable to concentrate.
> (Equality Act 2010, 2010)

If a child or young person has or is suffering CPTSD resulting in gaps in the pre-frontal cortex, then surely this child has a disability and needs support. How well are our schools currently informed of this and equipped to deal with this? Are schools simply stuck in the past and blaming the child for "chosen behaviour" over which they have little or no control?

I would like you to take part in a little quiz. Please indulge me. Below are three quotes with the dates removed. Take a few minutes to work out which years you think the quotes are from.

1. The General secretary for the National Association of Head Teachers said the judgement – which does not ban caning – will cause confusion in schools which will have to distinguish between children who are allowed to be beaten and those who are not.

   "You cannot have one section of pupils who may be subject to punishment and another section who cannot be punished," he said.

   "My advice to members is – carry on caning."
   (BBC, n.d.)

2. "You will each learn this table by heart over the next week, then I will test each of you in a random question and answer session next week. Anyone who can't answer or answers wrong will be strapped by me".

3. A BBC report from XXXX says the heads claimed that boys would be hit using "a thin, broad flat paddle to both buttocks simultaneously in a firm controlled manner." Meanwhile, "girls could be strapped on the hand and then comforted by a member of staff and encouraged to pray."
   (McInerney, 2017)

The answers may surprise you. The first quote is from 1982. The second 1950. The third is from 2005 where "the heads of a number of Christian fellowship independent schools appealed, at length, through various courts, for the ability to have delegated authority from parents to physically punish their children should they wish" (McInerney, 2017).

The reason I have included this quiz is because in the early 2000s some school leaders were still arguing for the right to physically punish children. I would hope that the vast majority of people reading this book can see how old fashioned and out of date such an approach was to school discipline. I also hope that because of reading this book, you will now begin to appreciate why our current way of thinking needs to be challenged and why *Relational Inclusion* is so important for educational success.

Stress

If we are truly to understand ourselves and the children and young people we work with, we must have a grasp of the different types of stress that we experience.

Positive Stress

Positive stress gives us a brief increase in our heart rate and mild elevations in our stress hormone levels. This is the kind of everyday stress we experience, and it is actually good for us. It helps us to perform well in important situations such as interviews or when we are under pressure. It challenges us to be the best version of ourselves. It gives us a shot of adrenaline which can help us when situations get difficult. It boosts our creative and critical thinking. It helps us to learn new things on the fly. Positive stress is a powerful tool that can help us have a positive response to an obstacle.

Tolerable Stress

Tolerable stress is a temporary stress response which helps us cope with some of the more difficult experiences of being human. It is often triggered by adversity or threat such as car accidents, death, serious illness or injury, national disasters, and acts of terrorism. This kind of stress is buffered by supportive adults and as long as someone is present, although unpleasant to experience, is usually not harmful.

Toxic Stress

Toxic stress is caused by prolonged activation of the stress response system. This is the steady and constant drip of physical or emotional abuse, chronic neglect, caregiver substance abuse or mental illness, or exposure to violence. Without protective adult relationships, toxic stress can result in CPTSD.

The Still Face Experiment

The Still Face Experiment was carried out in 1970 by Dr Ed Tronick. It provides a clear insight into how toxic stress starts to appear in just two minutes. The study involved a baby and a mother. It begins with a very normal and healthy interaction between the parent and her child. They are engaged in "serve and return" where, for example, the child points to something and the parent responds by looking in that direction. In the second part of the experiment, which is very hard to watch, the mother turns away, waits a moment, and then presents a "still face." They maintain a neutral, unresponsive expression, no matter what the baby does. The baby continues to test other sounds and movements to try and gain her mother's attention. Very quickly frustration sets in; the baby moves awkwardly, cries, and screeches. In the final part of the experiment the mother returns her attention to normal, and the relationship is quickly repaired.

The experiment shows how quickly a child's frustration builds and the impact that consistent, prolonged inattention has. If you then place a child in a classroom, we can see how a lack of parental responsiveness may impact on the child and how their frustration may be interpreted as "chosen behaviour." Children and young people may not yet have the words or vocabulary to describe their feelings. This doesn't mean however that the emotions aren't there. The children may start to "behave their feelings." In a baby this may be a screech or a cry. But as the child grows older the screech and cry may become stronger physical and emotional outbursts. When children do not get the responses they expect, need, and deserve, their brain quickly adapts. If this happens over a sustained period of time then the brain will make new neural networks, others will be lost, and the brain adapts to help the child survive the best way they can in the world that they inhabit.

What Is Trauma?

So, what is trauma? This is a very big question. Trauma is very much at the forefront of thinking in 2024. There are many books whose sole purpose is to discuss this, and the purpose of this book is not to explore the idea and psychology of trauma in great detail. It is, however, necessary to summarise what trauma is and isn't and why a basic understanding and awareness is so necessary for Relational Inclusion.

Trauma is not something that happens to you. "Trauma is what happens inside you as a result of what happens to you" (Mate & Mate, 2022). This means that although two people may be in the same place at the same time and physically experience the same thing, their emotional responses may be very different. It is also important to understand that because it seemingly doesn't affect one person, that doesn't mean it hasn't affected another. And to further complicate matters, the fact that is doesn't "seem" to have affected someone, doesn't mean it hasn't. It is vital that we recognise the fact that many children and young people (and adults) have experienced, are experiencing, and will experience trauma and it is our job to be aware of this and make our settings as aware of this as possible.

If we consider the brain as a massive filing system (which is a ridiculous simplification of a much more complicated process – but please follow my metaphor), when we experience something, our brain files it away neatly. It may be a memory or a smell or an emotion. Each experience has its place and is filed. However, when we experience trauma, our brain struggles to process and place it. This means that the trauma floats, it isn't "filed" anywhere. This also means when another experience occurs – again it may be a smell, or a sound, or a word, or just a feeling – the trauma will resurface and come straight back to the current thinking brain. The file has not been filed away; it remains to remind us that something is unsafe. It means we may re-live or re-experience the trauma as though it is happening in real time, right now, because of whatever re-triggered it.

Trauma is also often referred to as big "T" trauma and little "t" trauma which I will explain shortly. Interestingly I recently attended a talk where a trauma survivor complained about these terms. He said that trauma doesn't need a label. It doesn't matter whether the trauma is big or little, trauma is trauma, and to the person suffering this is a real, frightening, and life changing thing, no matter what the cause.

However, to understand trauma and its causes I think big "T" and little "t" are useful terms in helping us appreciate how widespread and varied trauma can be. Big "T" trauma refers to possibly more recognisable and obvious life-threatening events or situations. This could be a natural disaster, a violent crime, a school shooting, a serious car accident, the death of a parent, child abuse.

Little "t" trauma refers to less obvious and harder to recognise incidents. These are highly distressing events that affect individuals on a personal level. The events leading to this trauma tend to be non-life threatening in themselves. This could be bullying, the death of a pet, emotional abuse, a childhood experience, the breakdown of a relationship.

It is important to understand that you can "wound a kid not by doing bad things to them, but also by not meeting their needs. Even doting parents can easily, unknowingly, inflict small 't' traumas on their children" (Mate & Mate, 2022).

We need to be aware as much as possible whether a child is actively experiencing trauma – this means the trauma is still occurring, or they are in a trauma recovery stage – this means the trauma is in the past. In terms of intervention, if we confuse these two things we can cause more harm than good.

It is not our job in education to make judgements of the children and young people we work with in terms of their mental health and wellbeing. It is our job to make sure they have the best possible experience that we can provide. This means that we must be curious about their lives and their experiences and be empathetic in our help. As Atticus Finch says, "You never really understand a person until you consider things from his point of view – until you climb into his skin and walk around in it" (Lee, 1960).

To further complicate matters there is a large cross-over between the symptoms of trauma and attention deficit disorder (ADHD). In both cases children will have difficulty concentrating and learning in school; they will be easily distracted; they will often appear not to listen; they may seem disorganised, hypervigilant, and restless; they might have difficulty sleeping. It is really important that the right diagnosis is made. Mistaking ADHD for trauma could lead to medication which could mask the actual cause of the problem, pushing the trauma deeper into the subconscious.

Kline and Levine (2006) explain that "the essence of trauma is the urge to escape coupled with the perception of not being able to". This must be a truly terrifying place to live, and it is our duty to adapt our practice accordingly.

Mike – A Case Study

The case study below provides a real example of how an event which may appear innocuous to some, had long lasting effects on Mike.

Mike suffered with road rage. He had no idea where it came from but as soon as he got behind the wheel and another driver drove badly it was there. He was instantly seething. His jaws clenched, his eyes widened, and he was so angry at their poor choices and lack of road sense that he could quite literally kill. He fizzed with fury. It got so bad that his wife and small children were scared to travel with him. The language he used was atrocious. The threats he threw out were both intimidating and believable. And to make matters worse he had absolutely no control over what was happening or his accompanying behaviour. The red mist came down and he was lost in it.

He sought help from a trauma therapist and together they worked on an activity called "float back." This is an attempt to find the root cause of a traumatic experience.

Suddenly he was ten years old. He was sitting in a classroom and the teacher had asked him to read. Reading in front of the class wasn't anyone's idea of fun but it was one of those things they all had to do. He took a deep breath and started to read his paragraph.

Midway through the teacher interrupted him. In a mechanical voice, in front of the whole class, they said, "Why-are-you-reading-like-a-robot? That-is-not-how-we-read-out-loud."

The class burst out in fits of laughter. Young Mike felt his cheeks flush with shame. He wanted to stand up, to shout, to scream. But he was trapped in his chair and hot tears streamed down his cheeks.

His therapist explained that though unintentional, his teacher's admonishment and the ensuing shame he had felt meant that this incident had become a traumatic experience.

As an adult, behind the wheel of a car, he was experiencing the same feeling of shame, and this was causing him to re-experience his trauma. This was the loose file in the filing cabinet, reminding him of his unsafe feelings. However, he was no longer trapped in a classroom or silenced by shame and so all the pent-up rage, frustration, and humiliation he experienced and held inside as a 10-year-old boy was unleashed, with the power and strength of a 35-year-old man.

Our conscious and unconscious actions can have so much influence on those around us, especially when we are in a position of authority or power. It is important that, where possible, we are aware of the impact of our actions. As adults it is equally important to understand what makes us who we are and to understand why we behave the way we do.

Polyvagal Theory

In 1994, Dr Stephen Porges introduced Polyvagal Theory (Porges, 1995). His theory explores the role of the vagus nerve and the part it plays in emotion regulation. The vagus nerve is also known as the wandering nerve (vagus is Latin for "straying or wandering") as it is the longest nerve in the body, travelling from the brainstem to the gut – romantically linking the brain to the body.

Porges uses his theory to explain some of why we behave the way we do. According to the theory, shifts in the autonomic (involuntary) nervous system lead to three states.

The first state is our state of "social engagement." If we think in terms of a car, this is cruise control. Everything in our mind and body is fine. We are happy and content – we are "cruising." This is our optimal state for learning and engagement.

The second state is "fight" or "flight." If we continue our idea of a car, this is foot flat down – we are accelerating to get away. In Polyvagal Theory this state is also called mobilisation. This was discussed in more detail in Chapter 3.

Theory into Practice

When I worked in secondary mainstream, I didn't know any of this. When a fight broke out – which invariably they did from time to time – I used a certain strategy and now I know why it worked. Its success also relied on having safe and trusted relationships with the children and young people.

What I did was this. I would find a way into the scuffle without putting myself at too much risk. Then I would place my hand firmly on one of their shoulders. Now this is a fine balance – if you put your hand down too firmly it becomes threatening. The action needs to help them feel safe and secure.

When we fight, our amygdala takes control, and our thinking brain (pre-frontal cortex) shuts down. If we want to co-regulate a child, we need to get their thinking brain back online. We need to help the child come down from their hypervigilance, take their foot off the accelerator, and return to social engagement.

I would then whisper in their ear – and not in a weird way! I would say something like, "It's okay. I've got you. You're okay now. There is no trouble." I would avoid telling them to calm down; I wouldn't bombard them with instructions. I would keep my words simple and safe. Again, this helped to bring the thinking brain back online.

Sometimes I would say, "You can shout and swear – it's okay. We're going to walk this way." The use of humour can help if used correctly and the relationships are strong enough. This often led to a comedy moment where the child (and by child it would generally be a 15- or 16-year-old who towered above me) would do the pretend "let me at him" thing. They would make a pretend effort to keep fighting but generally by this point their intent on fighting had passed. When your hand is on someone's shoulder, you can feel the moment the tension passes. The amygdala has conceded power, and the thinking brain kicks back in.

The final state is "freeze." Again, in our car, this is the point that we slam on the breaks. We shut down and immobilise. Our bodies can only fight or run away for so long. Eventually, when we can't run anymore, we shut down.

There are many images and diagrams of Polyvagal Theory, and it is important to recognise that things can only happen in this order. We don't jump stages. We always go from one to two and finally to three. At each stage, our brain and nervous system work together to protect us from perceived danger. If we are in fight or flight, we are primed for battle or to escape. If we are in freeze, we shut down, our body plays dead (see Table 4.1).

For those of us who work with children and young people, understanding and being able to recognise this is crucial – not only in them, but in ourselves as well. When we are in those states we cannot learn or teach, and we are unable to listen to what everyone else may see as reason. We are either in high alert (hypervigilance) and our brain and body are focusing on escaping to survive, or we shut down (hypo-vigilance) and therefore unable to access anything other than the basics our bodies need to keep us alive.

Just think about those hair-raising moments where someone cuts you up on the motorway or someone slams their breaks on in front of you. Your heart pounds, your mouth goes dry, and you certainly can't think about or recall Shakespearian quotes or mathematical formulas.

Table 4.1 Hypo-vigilance or "Freeze"

This happens in our body:	This happens in our mind:
Our ears tune out so that we can't hear anything	We take on a dissociative state
Our breathing becomes very shallow or stops	We think nothing
Our heart slows right down	We blank out
We can't speak	Unconsciously we adapt another persona
We can't sense our body/it's like we're watching ourselves from above	We speak in a different voice
We have poor postural control	Our memory is selective or difficult to access
We become very still	

(Bombèr, 2020)

Neuroception

Dr Stephen Porges also coined the term "neuroception." Unlike perception, neuroception occurs outside of conscious thought. "Neuroception refers to the neural circuits that allow our bodies to register whether an environment is safe or dangerous" (Porges, 2004).

In other words, our brain is doing things we don't even realise. It is predicting what it expects to happen. "We don't respond to what happens, we respond to our perception of what happens" (Mate & Mate, 2022). For readers who have been around a few years, it's a bit like the Numbskulls from *The Beezer* comic. For those of you who haven't a clue what I'm talking about, think the film *Inside Out*. Most of the time, its predictions are accurate.

When we are under threat or hypervigilant, "neuroception" kicks in. Our brain predicts danger and defends us. This is a survival mechanism; however, it isn't always accurate. Many teachers and school leaders contact me and say, "and suddenly, out of nowhere, this child erupted." I must be gentle with my response. If you are unfortunate enough to have a "neutral" or an "angry resting 'bitch' face," a hypervigilant child is likely to interpret this as threat and dysregulate further. The adult may be totally unaware of their face and the child's response to it, and to them the incident appears to occur "out of nowhere." My advice here is to take a good look in the mirror and, if necessary, work on your facial expressions.

The extract below illustrates a clear example of neuroception:

> A FEW YEARS AGO, I received an e-mail from a man who served in the Rhodesian army in southern Africa in the 1970s, before the end of apartheid. He'd been drafted against his will, handed a uniform and a rifle, and ordered to hunt down guerrilla fighters. To make matters worse, before the draft, he'd been an advocate for the same guerrillas that he was now required to treat as the enemy.
>
> He was deep in the forest one morning, conducting practice exercises with his small squad of soldiers, when he detected movement ahead of him. With a pounding heart, he saw a long line of guerrilla fighters dressed in camouflage and carrying machine guns. Instinctively, he raised his rifle, flipped off the safety catch, squinted down the barrel, and aimed at the leader, who was carrying an AK-47 assault rifle.
>
> Suddenly, he felt a hand on his shoulder. "Don't shoot," whispered his buddy behind him. "It's just a boy." He slowly lowered his rifle, looked again at the scene, and was astonished by what he now saw: a boy, perhaps ten years old, leading a long line of cows. And the dreaded AK-47?
>
> It was a simple herding stick.
>
> For years afterward, this man struggled to understand the unsettling episode. How had he managed to mis-see what was right in front of his eyes and nearly kill a child?
>
> What was wrong with his brain?
>
> As it turns out, nothing was wrong with his brain. It was working exactly as it should have.
>
> (Barrett, 2021)

Attachment

John Bowlby and Mary Ainsworth were the pioneers of attachment theory. "This theory proposes that the emotional and social development of an infant is profoundly shaped by their relationship with their primary caregivers" (Main, 2023). To help understand attachment theory we must consider the basic needs of a baby. If a baby cries, how do we respond? We might rock the baby and sing to it. We might check the baby's nappy and change it. We might feed the baby. We might talk to the baby and change its environment, pointing things out to stimulate it. We might just cuddle the baby. We probably won't get it right all the time but if we generally meet the needs of the baby, this is good enough parenting, and the baby will be securely attached.

Ambivalent Attachment

Ambivalent attachment is easier to understand if we think of it as "on-off parenting." This means that sometimes the baby's needs are met and sometimes they are not. There is no pattern to when their needs will or won't be met and not surprisingly for the baby, this leaves them confused by an even more unpredictable world. Metaphorically they wonder if they are good enough, whether they can trust the world, why their trusted adult is not paying them enough attention. As the adult relationship is unreliable, they question whether they are valid.

Intermittent Reinforcement

A study was carried out with rats to test this. It was called intermittent reinforcement. To demonstrate secure attachment, rats were kept in a cage and fed through a pipe. The food was provided at regular times and the rats were content. To test the effects of "on-off parenting" the rats were fed peanuts intermittently. There was no pattern to when they would be fed. The rats became obsessed with the pipe. They could not settle or get on with their lives. They stayed around the pipe in the hope of being fed.

> If we transfer this into a classroom environment, ambivalent attached children are often very anxious. They are overly dependent of the teacher or TA and can appear helpless without an adult by their side. They struggle to work independently and are easily distracted. These can be the children who become the class clowns as they search for recognition. Often their verbal skills are more developed than their writing skills as they become adept at finding ways to get attention. They may appear work avoidant as they apply all sorts of strategies to gain attention such as arguing or generating discussion.
>
> (Delaney, 2017)

Interestingly we often refer to these children as attention seeking. If we reframed our language and thought about them as attachment or connection seeking, we might start to change our behaviour and approach to these kinds of children.

Ambivalent attachment is usually a result of parental separation or loss or work patterns leading to parental unavailability. To support these children in schools we must provide consistency. If they can have an emotionally available adult who they know has dedicated time for them, this will start to support their needs. If the adult can provide a daily time and place where they can meet the child, the child will begin to feel valid and their need for connection will be met. This approach must be delicate for the child's needs are sensitive. If the member of staff is going to be absent (and knows in advance) they must explain this to the child and, where possible, make an alternative arrangement with another trusted adult. Consistency and communication are absolutely key to supporting ambivalent attached children.

Avoidant Attachment

Avoidant attachment is easier to understand if we think of it as "off parenting." This means that the baby's needs are not met. These babies learn that adults aren't there for them. They realise very quickly that they have to do things for themselves as no-one else will do it for them. Emotional suppression replaces emotional regulation for they soon work out that crying doesn't bring them the attention they need.

These babies grow up to be children who don't avoid relationships (as the heading might suggest); instead, they avoid having feelings in relationships. In the classroom these children deny support from the teacher or TA. They are uncomfortable with teachers standing in close proximity. They want to complete tasks independently and either don't respond to direct verbal praise or respond badly to it. These children appear to be self-sufficient – often in schools we refer to them as being resilient. They may refuse to work with teaching assistants. Their verbal communication skills are often under-developed, and they lack emotion and empathy. When frustrated, they are more likely to rip up work than ask for help.

Unfortunately, this is very much not the case. Their internal working model tells them that they don't need help, that adults aren't there for them anyway. This can obviously cause many problems for them both with relationships and their working life. To support these children, we must stop trying to make direct contact with them. We should try to notice when they are engaged in work and then offer comments using depersonalised language. For example, we might say:

> Number 3 is a bit difficult. There is an example on the board.
> As opposed to saying:
> "I see you have found number 3 a bit difficult. Let me show you another example."
> We should find different ways of praising the child – and definitely avoid public praise. We should comment on the task, rather than the child's efforts.
>
> (Delaney, 2017)

Avoidant attachment is usually the result of either an emotionally unavailable parent, a depressed parent or an overly anxious parent.

Disorganised Attachment

Disorganised attachment is usually the result of severe neglect, violence, and/or abuse. These children often have high ACEs, are often our looked after children, and unfortunately are very often permanently excluded from school. These children experienced chaos as babies. They learned that the people who love them hurt them. They grow up thinking that chaos is normal and that you should hurt the people that you love.

> In the classroom these children change rapidly from being highly agitated to switching off. They get very frustrated and may bang their heads and punch things. They will often run out of the classroom unexpectedly and explode into temper for no apparent reason. They can be very abusive to the teacher and other children.
>
> (Delaney, 2017)

These are the children who will really "push our buttons." They may respond very warmly initially; we might put in lots of extra effort and really think we have succeeded where others have failed. And then suddenly they will seemingly throw it all back in our faces.

These children have no confidence or self-esteem. They have no secure base. They will try to make us hate them. Yet these children need us most. They need to know that we will be there. We need to help them understand that the world doesn't hurt, and that people can be safe; we need to provide clear routines and structures, and we need a team of people to wrap around them whilst also supporting each other through this very difficult and challenging process.

Promoting a comprehensive understanding of the ongoing needs of children with complex behaviours and advocating for inclusive and well-informed support structures within educational settings are critical steps towards ensuring the well-being and success of all students, regardless of their challenge. The bulk of this chapter outlines some of the many issues our children may be experiencing. In schools, we are aware of some, scratching the surface with others, and possibly blind to many more.

Internal Inclusion/Exclusion and Isolation Rooms

At this point I would like to draw attention to the use of "internal inclusion/exclusion units" in mainstream schools. In my experience they have many different names and many different ways of operating. I think that most schools would see them as a resource to ensure that teachers are allowed to teach, students to learn, and those with additional learning needs to be supported. Part of the problem with these "units" is that there is no clear understanding of what support these children need and how this support can be provided. There isn't an agreed set of standards by which these facilities can be judged, and it is my belief that they are often set up with a deficit model in mind that focuses on the needs of the majority, not the needs of those who struggle with behaviour regulation. The children are not supported in developing a sense of self – or agency.

In the past, I have been asked by a mainstream headteacher to provide some training for the staff for an inclusion unit that they were setting up. I asked the staff what their brief was, and they explained that they were to have the child for a period of 12 weeks, and they were then to be returned to the main part of the school when they "had learned how to behave." I wished them "good luck." Again, the problem with this model is the misconception that all schools need to do is to give some pupils intensive training on how to behave and they will then be ready to return to the main school and become model citizens. I hope this chapter has illustrated that our children are facing far more complexity in their lives and that this can't be "solved" in a short space of time.

I don't know how this provision developed or how successful the initiative was, but I have seen the same scenario many times before. I believe they are created with the best intention but without the knowledge, experience, and understanding to make them actually succeed. What happens, inevitably, is that the children are initially reluctant to go into the unit but then find that the staff have been specially selected as they can work with complex students. They get plenty of attention and have their needs met. They feel a sense of belonging and begin to enjoy their time in this provision. Relationships are built and then the time comes for them to "go back into mainstream." We gradually, or sometimes suddenly, remove all of the support structures and expect them to have "learned their lesson." They go back into the main part of the school, which has not changed, and the pupil again is faced with the member of staff who they did not get on well with in the first place, who does not know how to meet their needs and, in some cases, does not like them, and we are back to square one. To make matters worse, the school believe they have made reasonable adjustments, done all they possibly can, and the child is blamed and often punished through further suspension or permanent exclusion.

A Note about Specialist Provision

The principle of "follow the money," as noted in the film *All the President's Men*, suggests that financial trails can uncover underlying realities, including instances of political corruption. This concept can be extended to gauge the true priorities and values of individuals, organisations, and societies based on how and where they allocate their financial resources.

In education, and more specifically special education, this principle offers a lens through which to examine the allocation of resources and the inherent values such allocations reveal about those who allocate the funding.

Education budgets are constantly under scrutiny, with the need to allocate funds wisely being a constant pressure. This has become especially important with the significant rise in spending on children with mental health needs. The number of pupils assessed as needing an Education, Health and Care Plan (EHCP) has risen significantly in recent years. As mentioned in Chapter 1, the percentage of all children with an EHCP in England has risen from 2.8 percent in 2015/16 to 4.8 percent in 2022/23 (Gov.uk, 2024).

My point in raising this is not to moan about the lack of state funding for education but rather to spotlight the underlying misconceptions surrounding the education of children with complex behavioural issues. By doing so, I aim to explore how these misconceptions influence the support provided to any child exhibiting challenging behaviours and how they are perceived.

Are They "Better" Yet?

During my years of hosting school visits, many visitors have observed children learning and behaving positively in their classrooms. This often prompts the question: "Why couldn't these children be educated in a mainstream school?" The key to the success of these children in learning and behaving well lies in the fact that their specific needs are being understood and then effectively met.

I believe that a significant number of these children could indeed thrive in a mainstream school setting, provided that the schools continue to address and fulfil their individual needs. The implication of the initial question is that they are now "fixed," and mainstream is cheaper provision!

This highlights a crucial issue concerning the misunderstandings surrounding children with complex needs and the challenges institutions face in meeting these needs effectively. The notion that children receiving specialised support should, over time, require less funding due to perceived improvements in behaviour is flawed.

The reality of the situation is, of course, very different. These children have complex needs when they come to us and they will still have those needs when they leave. Whilst they may develop coping mechanisms and improve their behaviour, it does not imply that they have been "fixed" and no longer face any challenges.

Reflection

- As school leaders, do we have a clear understanding of trauma and attachment and how is this reflected in our policy and practice?
- Are our staff trained to recognise when our children and young people are in their social engagement state and are ready to learn or to recognise fight or flight and have strategies to support co-regulation?
- Are we training our staff to understand neuroception so that we can have a better insight into the way some of our children and young people respond?
- Are we doing all we can to prevent retraumatisation?

We can all think of traumatic times in our lives which have impacted greatly on our mental health, such as the death of a parent. Over time it does get easier, but it never leaves us. There may well be times in our lives, even many years later, when something brings it all flooding back and we again find it difficult to deal with the emotions.

To know how to help children to develop the skills to better navigate the world they live in we need to look at the neuroscience and to challenge some of the misconceptions, such as that the child can be fixed in 12 weeks or that they are choosing to behave badly. From the earliest years relationships with others determine how our brain develops. If a child suffers some major trauma, then their brain adapts to help the child survive. Neural networks are built and strengthened if this trauma happens over a prolonged period of time. The adapted brain can then cause the child problems when dealing with very ordinary situations, such making new friends or meeting a new teacher. The child may mis-read situations, the child may find things more stressful, and their behaviour may seem inappropriate. Even the language associated with the more complex children needs to be addressed. They are seen as "repeat offenders."

This is not something that can be undone in 12 weeks or by explaining the rules and expectations clearly. I am not saying that this child cannot be helped or that we should just allow the perceived "bad behaviour" to continue. What I am saying is that if we do not try to understand what lies behind the behaviours then we risk adding further trauma. Shouting at a child, putting them into isolation, or suspending them from school will do nothing to rebuild the neural networks. This is like shouting at a child in a wheelchair because they can't navigate the stairs. We need to adapt the environment to help these children to succeed.

Anyone who has got a deep-rooted fear or anxiety will tell you that to face that fear is a daunting prospect and not something we relish. Many of us prefer avoidance rather than facing the fear. Many children who find school, relationships, and everyday situations stressful may well choose to avoid the situation altogether and stay at home in their rooms. Others will try to navigate the world in the only way that they know how and when they make mistakes, which they will, they need to be helped by people who show them respect and understanding.

When someone contacts me from a school when they are dealing with a child that has behaved very badly, they often want the student to be taken away as they are very stressed and don't know what to do.

They expect someone to "deal" with the problem. There are some things that can be done to help the child at that point but taking them away is not going to prevent a similar situation arising with another child in the future. That is where we need fundamental system change so that schools adapt their environments to better meet the needs of all children, even those who find it difficult to regulate their behaviour. This is not something that is going to happen overnight. This is something that will take time and consistency and which should start from an early age. It will need to continue throughout their school lives and probably beyond. The trauma will always be there, and they can't be "fixed" but they can live healthy and productive lives and contribute fully to society.

It can be done. More and more, we are seeing the use of the sunflower lanyards to signal that a person may have a hidden disability. We have theatres and cinemas which have "relaxed" performances for those who would otherwise struggle. Recently I witnessed a very encouraging situation at an airport that really made me feel proud to be part of the human race. I arrived at the gate to wait for the flight and sat opposite a gentleman who was walking with a stick and was wearing the sunflower lanyard. He arrived at the same time as me and was clearly struggling. After a wait of around half an hour the staff announced that there was a gate change, and we had to relocate back to where we had started. The gentleman clearly became distressed and angry. Seeing the lanyard stopped the staff in their tracks and they sat down beside him and explained that they would make arrangements for him to be transferred and that he just needed to sit tight. One member of staff stayed with him and talked to him gently. The next time I saw him he was sitting on the plane looking calm and happy. Sadly, there was going to be a further delay; the ground crew had not yet even picked up the cases to be loaded onto the plane. Before this announcement came over the tannoy, one of the cabin crew sat beside him and explained the problem and some options that were available to him. Again, he relaxed, and it appeared that he had a positive experience on the flight.

In this scenario, as a result of effective training, staff were able to take time to understand disability and they then made reasonable adjustments. If schools continue to see poor behaviour as a wilful act instead of understanding how some children will struggle with behaviour regulation, then we will never make any progress. If schools only deal with the crisis instead of proactively putting structures in place to help all our children build resilience, then we will all be worse off. Making reasonable adjustments benefits the whole of society. When a building installs automatic sliding doors to assist those who are in a wheelchair, they also benefit a parent with a buggy, people with their arms full of shopping bags, and old aged pensioners and nobody complains that the adjustment is not needed.

As L.R. Knost (child development researcher) says:

There are **no bad children**.
There are bad choices.
There are bad moments.
There are bad days.
There are bad situations.
But there are **no bad children**.

References

Barrett, L. F. (2021). *Seven and a half lessons about the brain*. Picador.
BBC. (n.d.). *On this day.* http://news.bbc.co.uk/onthisday/low/dates/stories/february/25/newsid_2516000/2516621.stm
Bombèr, L. M. (2020). *Know me to teach me*. Worth Publishing.
Chugani, H. T., Behen, M. E., Muzik, O., Juhász, C., Nagy, F. & Chugani, D. C. (2001, December). Local brain functional activity following early deprivation: A study of postinstitutionalized Romanian orphans. *NeuroImage, 14*(6), 1290–1301. https://doi.org/10.1006/nimg.2001.0917
Delaney, M. (2017). *Attachment for teachers*. Worth Publishing.
Equality Act 2010. (2010). *The national archives*. https://www.legislation.gov.uk/ukpga/2010/15/contents
Glasper, E. A. (2020, March 16). Romania's forgotten children: sensory deprivation revisited. *Comprehensive Child and Adolescent Nursing, 43*(2), 81–87. https://doi.org/10.1080/24694193.2020.173525
Gov.uk. (2024, June 20). *Special educational needs in England*. Explore Education Statistics. https://explore-education-statistics.service.gov.uk/find-statistics/special-educational-needs-in-england
Herman, J. (1992). Complex PTSD: A syndrome in survivors of prolonged and repeated trauma. *Journal of Traumatic Stress, 5*(3), 377–391.
Jones, B. D. (2012, June). Shell shocked. *American Psychological Association*. https://www.apa.org/monitor/2012/06/shell-shocked
Kline, M. & Levine, P. A. (2006). *Trauma through a child's eyes: Awakening the ordinary miracle of healing?*. North Atlantic Books.
Lee, H. (1960). *To kill a mockingbird*. Cornerstone.

Main, P. (2023, June 30). *Bowlby's attachment theory*. Structural Learning. https://www.structural-learning.com/post/bowlbys-attachment-theory

Mate, G. & Mate, D. M. (2022). *The myth of normal*. Ebury.

McInerney, L. (2017, January 25). *When did schools ban corporal punishment?* Schools Week. https://schoolsweek.co.uk/when-did-schools-ban-corporal-punishment/

Office for Health Improvement and Disparities. (2022, November 2). *Working definition of trauma-informed practice*. Gov.uk. https://www.gov.uk/government/publications/working-definition-of-trauma-informed-practice/working-definition-of-trauma-informed-practice

Porges, S. W. (1995). Orienting in a defensive world: Mammalian modifications of our evolutionary heritage. *A Polyvagal Theory. Psychophysiology, 32*(4), 301–318. https://doi.org/10.1111/j.1469-8986.1995.tb01213.x

Porges, S. W. (2004). *Neuroception: A subconscious system for detecting threats and safety*. https://chhs.fresnostate.edu/ccci/documents/07.15.16%20Neuroception%20Porges%202004.pdf

Santayana, G., (1905). *The life of reason: The phases of human progress (Vol. 1: Reason in common sense)*. Charles Scribner's Sons.

The National Archives. (n.d.). *"Shell shock" cases*. https://www.nationalarchives.gov.uk/education/resources/medicine-on-the-western-front-part-two/shell-shock-cases/

Chapter 5

The Lost Children

Working in schools is tough. There is never enough money. There is never enough time. The curriculum changes; the exam system changes; the ways we are judged changes; there is constant pressure. The one thing that doesn't change are the children and with children comes behaviour. It becomes hard to not apportion blame. This "bad behaviour" which, at times, makes a hard job almost impossible, must come from somewhere; it must be someone's fault. I used to blame the children, and I used to blame the parents. The children must certainly be aware and in control of their actions. And if they aren't managing their behaviour then it must be the fault of poor parenting.

Now that we know about neuroscience and the nervous system, we know that children aren't consciously choosing their behaviour quite in the way we previously thought. We also know that the vast majority of parents do the best they know how to for their children. If we are going to make a difference, if we are really going to change the way things work, then we must stop laying blame.

We must avoid using the deficit narrative which has been present in schools and society since the middle of the twentieth century. It's a perspective which blames failures in achievement and learning on the child. It implies that they fail because of a lack of effort or some kind of deficiency as opposed to recognising the failures or limitations of the education and training system. Deficit narratives imply that the children, not the schools or programmes, need to change in order to improve outcomes and experiences.

In the words of Charles Dickens, we must "have a heart that never hardens, and a temper that never tires and a touch that never hurts." We must do all we can to really understand the story behind the behaviour. This chapter will explore how we can gain a forensic understanding of what the children and young people are carrying with them beneath the surface.

***

When I got my first deputy headship the assistant head had a list on her wall of *lost boys*. This stayed in my mind. Maybe it was just because of *Peter Pan* or *The Lost Boys* (the vampire movie) or maybe she had hit on something that really resonated. For her, *the lost boys* were the children everyone overlooked. They weren't in school for a variety of reasons, and everyone was so busy either tracking progress or dealing with misbehaviour that those who just weren't there were simply overlooked. She was right to think about "the lost boys," although it shouldn't have just been the boys. In every school I have worked at since, I've thought about "the lost children."

In the last chapter I talked about children not being broken. What if we thought of these children as being lost? Some are literally lost in the system; some are ever present, but we still can't see them. At least, not behind the facade which is often disguised by perceived misbehaviour. In society, if someone is lost, we do all we can to find them. I think we should do all we can to "find" our lost children, to understand the story behind the behaviour. However, understanding the story alone isn't enough. Once we understand the story, what are we going to do differently? I have spent the last three years developing a *tool* and a supporting strategy to help us "see" the child behind the behaviour and develop a new way forward. As I explained in my guiding principles, *if a child could do better, then they would*. The "Pupil Profile Tool" (PPT) has been designed to help. It provides schools with a forensic understanding of their students including ACEs, trauma, attachment, and why these are so important.

It is important to recognise that although the PPT comprises of a series of questions, this is not a check-list activity. If it is used simply to tick boxes, we will never unlock the hidden story. The responses we gather to the questions help us piece together an insight into what might be hiding behind a child's behaviour. The more time we take to explore and the more detail we can provide, the clearer the picture becomes and subsequently we can provide a better quality of support. The tool is not something that is completed alongside parents or their children. We are not expecting staff to act as therapists. We are using it as a way of using the information we already have about our young people so that we can better understand and then support their needs.

A primary head teacher phoned me recently. I have spent the last year working with him on how we can support schools across the authority to adopt a more Relationally Inclusive approach. He asked if he could talk through a student who was behaving in a way that he'd not seen before as he wasn't quite sure what to do next. For me, the fact that he has already started to think that there might be another way to look at this is a sign that thought patterns and approaches can change.

He went on to describe a child who had never displayed difficulties and had no behaviour issues in lessons. He said he had a good relationship with the family and had known them for 15 years. He said the problems had started last term when the child was caught vaping in the toilets. He explained that previously he would have suspended the child; however, thinking through a different lens he would approach this differently. He spoke to the child and the family and reinforced the school's expectations. He recognised that a suspension was unlikely to have any impact.

A few weeks later, the child brought a Lego car to "show and tell." He proudly talked about his toy to the rest of his class. It then transpired that he had stolen the car from a local supermarket and the act had been caught on camera. When challenged, the child denied this had happened and said that a man had given him the car. When he was told that the headteacher had seen the footage of him stealing, he was unremorseful.

Again, the headteacher avoided the temptation to punish the child through suspension and opted for discussion. During the next half term, graffiti appeared in two places on the school walls. Camera footage showed the same boy to be responsible. Once again, the boy denied knowledge, was unremorseful, and tried to blame "some other boys."

This time the head did suspend. However, he also recognised that suspension was unlikely to change this escalating behaviour. The boy remained a model student in class. It was at this point the headteacher called me.

We can speculate as to what might be going on here. At the very least the child appears to be trying to attract attention to himself. The fact that when he gets the attention, he denies any involvement in the alleged incident might suggest that whilst he recognises something doesn't feel right and that he wants to be noticed, he doesn't understand why (he is only a primary child) and he doesn't quite know what to do with the attention.

The reason for this anecdote is to highlight the importance of finding the story behind the behaviour and one way to do this is to use the PPT. An alternative would be to escalate punitive measures until either the child does something so serious that they end up in the juvenile system or they are permanently excluded. Neither of these solutions will resolve whatever issues the child is carrying. If we profile the student with the intention of better understanding them and then employ a therapeutic rather than a punitive approach, we might stop this child simply becoming another behavioural statistic.

The rest of this chapter is divided into three sections.

- The first introduces the PPT and provides some background and explanation
- The second provides an example of the PPT in action and what we can learn
- The third explores the idea of a "PSHE Emotional Curriculum" and how core competencies can be used with children and young people

Section 1 – The Pupil Profile Tool

Part 1 – Adverse Childhood Experiences (ACEs) and Adverse Community Environments

In Chapter 2 I discussed ACEs in terms of staff and training. It is also useful to have an understanding of the number and type of ACEs our young people carry. This is because of the reasons outlined below:

- **Adversity leads to a damaged stress response**, which leads to toxic stress, which itself is the driver for a whole host of negative biological impacts and disease states
- Childhood adversity is associated with a variety of diseases and conditions in children that can be observed as early as infancy. In babies, exposure to ACEs is associated with growth delay, cognitive delay, and sleep disruption. **School-aged children show higher rates of asthma and poorer response to asthma rescue medicine, greater rates of infection, and more learning difficulties and behavioural problems,** and adolescents exhibit higher rates of obesity, bullying violence, smoking, teen pregnancy, teen paternity, and other risky behaviours such as early sexual activity
- **For every ACE a child has, the risk of tolerable stress tipping over into toxic stress increases,** as the system responds more frequently and intensely to multiple stressors

- When children have experienced adversity there are *measurable changes* to the brain structures (MRI scans)
- Two of the most common issues relating to adversity are **obesity and learning or behaviour problems**
- Patients with four or more ACEs were *twice* as likely to be overweight or obese and *32.6 times* more likely to have been diagnosed with learning and behaviour problems
- Kids who are struggling in school were being told that they had ADHD or a "behaviour problem" when these problems were directly correlated with toxic doses of adversity

(Burke Harris, 2018)

Pupil Profile Tool – ACEs

The more detail that can be provided with each question that applies, the better.

For each question, consider whether school is aware of a parent or other adult in the household who, in their interactions with the child, often or very often …

1. Committed sexual abuse
2. Committed physical abuse
3. Committed emotional abuse
4. Caused neglect

Has the child:

5. Suffered medical trauma
6. Witnessed a natural or man-made disaster
7. Witnessed family violence
8. Been a victim of family violence
9. Witnessed community or school violence
10. Witnessed or been a victim of criminal activity
11. Been affected by war or terrorism
12. Had a disruption in care giving or attachment losses
13. Suffered attachment losses
14. Witnessed or been a victim of parent criminal behaviour

Part 2 – Stress Response

Once we have an idea of the ACEs that might be affecting the child's story, it is then worth considering what happens "when" and "how" the child arrives to school. If we look at their actions through a relational and inclusive lens as opposed to seeing their actions as chosen defiance, it helps us better understand their story. Part 2 of the PPT considers arrival to school.

Pupil Profile Tool – Stress Response – Arrival

The more detail that can be provided with each question that applies, the better.
  Does the child often arrive:

1. Early
2. Late
3. Dysregulated
4. Hungry
5. Tired
6. Wearing inappropriate clothing
7. Complaining of illness
8. With poor personal hygiene

Part 3 – Hyperarousal

The theory behind stress response and hyperarousal was discussed in Chapter 3. When it comes to hyperarousal it is impossible not to recognise the cross-over between trauma and ADHD. Symptoms for both include a difficulty in concentrating and learning at school, being easily distracted, often seeming to not listen, disorganisation, hyperactivity, and restlessness. These are also characteristics that are sometimes seen as chosen behaviours and can be met with rigid punitive measures. Sometimes these children are labelled with "persistent disruptive behaviour."

> **Pupil Profile Tool – Stress Response – Hyperarousal**
>
> The more detail that can be provided with each question that applies, the better.
>
> Does the child or young person demonstrate any of the following?
>
> Please identify frequency in terms of hourly/daily/weekly.
>
> If you can pinpoint specific times or lessons that would also be useful.
>
> 1. Over-active responses
> 2. Defensive talk
> 3. Verbal outbursts
> 4. Physical outbursts
> 5. Violence towards other students
> 6. Violence towards adults
> 7. Exiting
> 8. Running away
> 9. Hiding
> 10. Refusal

Part 4 – Hypo-Arousal

Hypo-arousal was discussed in Chapter 4. I spent many years as a classroom teacher telling members of my form or class that they needed to go to bed earlier and stop playing whichever console they had. Some of them were often tired and would try to put their heads on the desk. I am not making excuses for teenage behaviour. Some teenagers do stay up too late. Equally some children are tired for an entirely different reason. It is hard work being in a constant state of hyperarousal. Equally our nervous system can only survive this way for so long and then it simply shuts down – this is hypo-arousal and it is vital we recognise what this might look like.

> **Pupil Profile Tool – Stress Response – Hypo-Arousal**
>
> The more detail that can be provided with each question that applies, the better.
> Does the child or young person demonstrate any of the following?
> Please identify frequency in terms of hourly/daily/weekly.
> If you can pinpoint specific times or lessons that would also be useful.
>
> 1. Day dreaming
> 2. Rocking
> 3. Making odd sounds
> 4. Using a different voice
> 5. Taking on a different persona
> 6. Being floppy
> 7. Not being with it
> 8. Risk taking
> 9. Unable to stand
> 10. Collapsing

Part 5 – Risk Behaviours

The "risk behaviours" listed below are high tariff behaviours and are often met with the consequence of permanent exclusion. In Chapter 6, I will explore vocabulary and although these are unarguably serious behavioural issues, it is still necessary to discover what the picture behind them might be. As Bruce Perry and Oprah Winfrey discuss at length, we must begin with the question *What Happened to You?*, rather than *What's Wrong with You?* (Perry & Winfrey, 2021).

> **Pupil Profile Tool – Risk Behaviours**
>
> The more detail that can be provided with each question that applies, the better.
> Are you aware of the child or young person's involvement of any of the following?

1. Child sexual exploitation (CSE) (at risk of/involved in)
2. Child criminal exploitation (CCE) (at risk of/involved in)
3. County lines (at risk of/involved in)
4. Fire setting
5. Substance use
6. Drug dealing
7. Oppositional
8. Overly sexualized behaviour
9. Racism
10. Sexism/homophobia
11. Carrying of or use of weapons
12. Theft
13. Non-violent vandalism
14. Anxiety/depression
15. Self-harm
16. Anger (lack of self-control)
17. Bullying
18. Being bullied

Part 6 – Attachment

Attachment theory and strategies to support children and young people are discussed in Chapter 4. I would just like to reiterate that it can be easy to mistake these children for being either attention seeking, resilient, or defiant.

Pupil Profile Tool – Ambivalent Attachment (On/Off Parenting)

The more detail that can be provided with each question that applies, the better.

1. Often anxious/overly dependent on staff
2. Acts helpless/stuck without adult support
3. Unable to work independently
4. Needs constant reassurance
5. Easily distracted
6. Continually looking for teacher

7. Easily upset if loses the teacher's attention
8. Engages in strategies to avoid work
9. Verbal skills more advanced than written

Pupil Profile Tool – Attachment (Off Parenting)

The more detail that can be provided with each question that applies, the better.

1. Denies support and help from staff
2. Doesn't want staff standing in close proximity
3. Apparent indifference to anxiety in new situation
4. May refuse to work with a TA
5. Wants to do tasks independently
6. Frustrated/destroys work rather than asking for help
7. Limited use of verbal communication
8. Limited creativity
9. Reacts badly to direct verbal praise

Pupil Profile Tool – Disorganised Attachment

The more detail that can be provided with each question that applies, the better.

1. Changes rapidly – very agitated to switched off
2. Gets very frustrated – bangs their heads/punches
3. Runs around uncontrollably
4. Runs out of class unexpectedly
5. Explodes into temper for no apparent reason
6. Can be very abusive to teacher or other children

Section 2 – The Pupil Profile Tool in Action

As headteachers and senior leaders we all develop our quirks. I haven't met a single headteacher who hasn't. One of mine is automatically asking the "so what?" question. I don't mean it unkindly, and I try applying the same question to my own thinking. I suppose we are bombarded with so many ideas, new initiatives, waffle, and nonsense that we have to filter all the information into things that will actually make a difference as opposed to things that just take up more time.

I find it slightly frustrating when people apply the "so what?" question to my thinking, mainly because I should have asked it first. When I first showed my colleagues the PPT they said, "That looks wonderful but *so, what?*"

It took me time to gather the evidence to back up the answer I had in my head. I am now in a position to answer the "so what" question confidently. To use the tool does take careful training. If it is used simply as a checklist to count as evidence to validate punitive consequences, we are massively missing a trick.

The next part of this chapter provides an example of the information the tool generates. It creates a series of layers of information. These layers, once pieced together, begin to tell us a story. They then pose a different question. If we know this information and understand why things escalate in the way that they do, can we continue to justify permanent exclusion? For this is ultimately what generally happens to the children displaying these behaviours. Can we continue to allow persistent disruptive behaviour to be a valid reason for permanent exclusion? Don't we have a duty of care to do things differently?

We profiled 92 key stage two primary school children who had been identified as being a potential risk for permanent exclusion with a tendency for persistent disruptive behaviour. They were not at immediate risk but had been identified as children who would likely be at risk if something didn't change. The next few pages draw together some of the findings.

Layer 1 – ACEs

Figure 5.1 shows the distribution of known ACEs across the cohort sampled.

The top 3 ACEs from this sample are:

- Disruption in care giving
- Witness to family violence
- Parent carer mental health

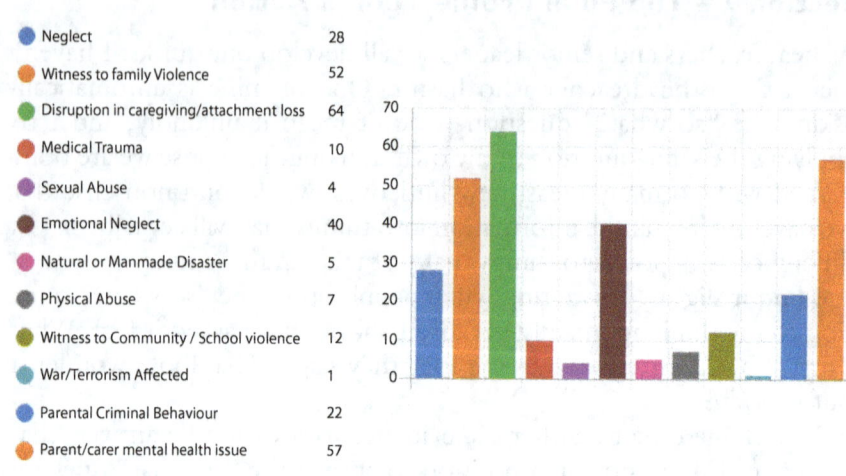

Neglect	28
Witness to family Violence	52
Disruption in caregiving/attachment loss	64
Medical Trauma	10
Sexual Abuse	4
Emotional Neglect	40
Natural or Manmade Disaster	5
Physical Abuse	7
Witness to Community / School violence	12
War/Terrorism Affected	1
Parental Criminal Behaviour	22
Parent/carer mental health issue	57

Figure 5.1 Distribution of ACEs across the Sampled Cohort.

The "So What..."

As a result of these three ACEs the children are likely to feel confused as the parenting they experience may be inconsistent. They could be receiving mixed messages which will confuse their outlook on the world. They will probably find it hard to trust. For these children dysregulation is normalised behaviour; their perspective of what is normal is distorted so they will seek to replicate this or mimic these behaviours as this is what is most familiar and they "believe" to be comfortable. Their internal working model (character blueprint) will develop to mirror their experience. They may seek unhealthy or inconsistent relationships. They may be triggered by minor things personal to their situation.

These children are "actively experiencing their trauma." Therefore, they need support in how to cope rather than a trauma recovery plan.

What Helps

- Safety and predictability (visual timetables work really well for these children)
- Consistency
- Reassurance that they know what is coming next
- Notice of change
- Grounding techniques which don't require keeping still

What Hinders

- If these symptoms are misdiagnosed as SEN, the child will be pathologised and potentially medicated unnecessarily
- Consequences that are too far away; for example if an incident occurs on a Monday and the consequence is enforced later in the week, the child won't link what happened to the consequence so they will be unable to adapt their behaviour should the same thing occur in the future
- Loud noises (voices or doors banging)
- Being singled out
- Working with new people without notice

Layer 2 – Stress Response

Figure 5.2 shows the distribution of "stress response – arrival" across the cohort sampled.

The top three effects of stress response on arrival to school from this sample are:

- Being tired
- Late arrival
- Complaining of illness

The "So What..."

Unsurprisingly these children are tired. This is because their bodies are flooded with adrenaline and cortisol which prevents them from settling. Linked to this, they are often late to school. When they do arrive

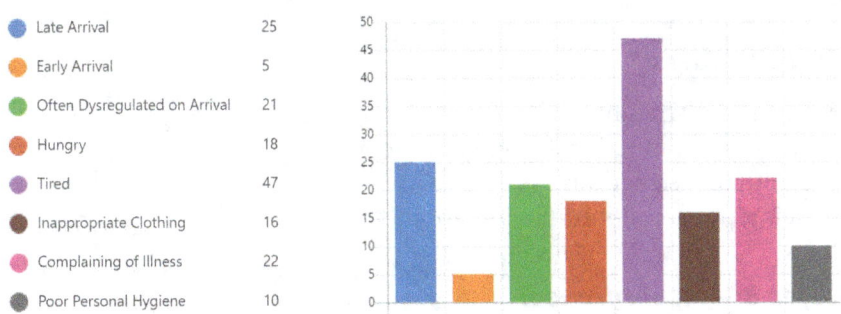

Figure 5.2 Distribution of Stress Response across the Cohort.

at school they are complaining of illness or displaying dysregulated behaviour. It is possible complaining of illness is a somatic response to the dysregulation they are experiencing. "Their bodies remember what their minds try to forget" (often attributed to Bessell van der Kolk).

> Somatic anxiety is the physical manifestation of anxiety. This can feel like a headache, tight shoulders, upset stomach, or fatigue. These symptoms are caused by the body's fight-or-flight response being constantly activated.
>
> (Pedersen, 2022)

It may be tempting to punish these children for being late or disorganised without understanding the ACEs behind this behaviour. Often schools address lateness by offering rewards or certificates for improved attendance. This incentive is unlikely to work with this cohort of children, potentially demotivating them, as they have no chance of succeeding with this type of approach. This may reinforce their internal working model's thought pattern of "I am not enough." If we are going to truly help children improve their attendance and punctuality, we must change our approach.

What Helps

- A supported transition from home to school in the morning
- This means time, space, food, drink, warmth, and grounding techniques – a bespoke toolbox created by the child
- An emotionally available adult (this doesn't need to be the same person as they need to learn that all adults are reliable)
- Transitional objects (things that remind them of a place of safety)

What Hinders

- Being put straight into a lesson or form-time
- Noise and unpredictable environments
- Multiple instructions
- Being pressured into talking about "why"

Layer 3 – Hyperarousal

Figure 5.3 shows how hyperarousal is displayed by the cohort sampled.

The Lost Children 115

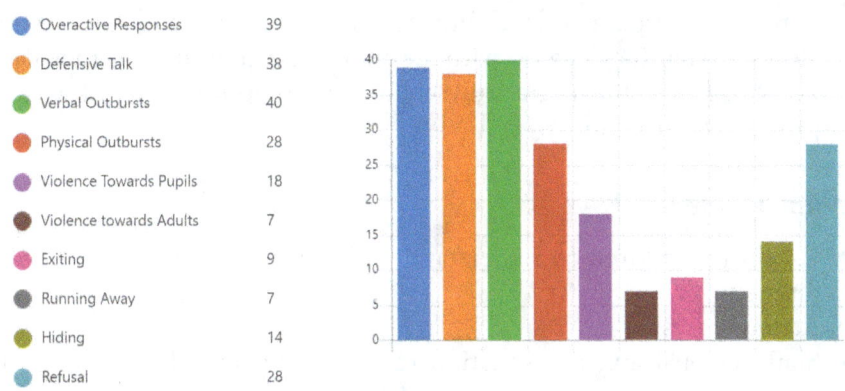

● Overactive Responses	39
● Defensive Talk	38
● Verbal Outbursts	40
● Physical Outbursts	28
● Violence Towards Pupils	18
● Violence towards Adults	7
● Exiting	9
● Running Away	7
● Hiding	14
● Refusal	28

Figure 5.3 How Hyperarousal Is Displayed by the Cohort.

The top three ways hyperarousal is displayed by this cohort are:

- Verbal outbursts
- Over-active responses
- Defensive talk

The "So What…"

As a result of the ACEs and initial stress response, these children demonstrate over-active responses, defensive talk, and verbal outburst. Once again, this could be perceived as chosen disruptive behaviour if the stages before haven't been recognised. These behaviours are not surprising as a dysregulated child will use skills which have worked in the past to get to safety. We may not agree with their method of behaviour; however this is a part of their survival instinct – if their nervous system has triggered fear, they will use any behaviour necessary to feel safe.

What Helps

- The child is operating from their amygdala. They need co-regulating to bring the pre-frontal cortex back on-line before they can engage academically
- In a classroom they need to feel genuinely included and wanted
- Music and rhythm can help (e.g. butterfly tapping)
- We need to meet these children where they are at rather than expecting them to meet the school requirements. This means moving away

from a one-size-fits-all approach towards a personalised understanding of their proximal development. In other words, we need to be clear on what they can do without help, compared to what they can do with help, applying a truly child-centred approach to allow for productive struggle

What Hinders

- Expecting children to understand and repair their mistakes at this moment
- Raised voices
- Staff personalising the situation (this is not about the member of staff)
- Multiple adult involvement

Layer 4 – Risk Behaviours

Figure 5.4 shows the risk behaviours of the cohort sampled.

The top risk behaviours displayed by this cohort are:

- Anxiety/depression
- Anger and a lack of self-control
- Bullying
- Oppositional
- Self-harm

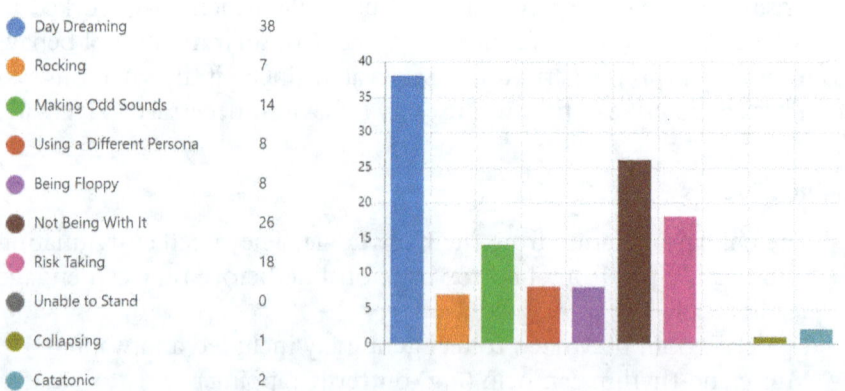

Figure 5.4 Risk Behaviours of the Sampled Cohort.

The "So What..."

Once again it is so important to highlight that if we just looked at these risk behaviours, we might make an assumption that these children are naughty, disruptive, and challenging and that they need firm discipline to learn the error of their ways. But firm discipline is not going to work. The very nature of childhood development is that it is a sequence of events: Sitting, crawling, walking, running, and jumping. If we miss a stage, we must go back and complete it in order to move forward.

We can see from the PPT that there is a clear sequence behind what might be causing their behaviour; this sequence is shown by layers one to three. Layer four is often the tip of the iceberg. It is also often the tipping point for schools, leading to behaviour that on the surface may be unforgiveable and unrepairable. The PPT helps us to start to understand the story behind their behaviour. Is it fair to punish a child for their layer four behaviours when we may have failed to recognise layers one, two, and three? Surely, we must try to support them along their journey. "If a child could do better, then they would." They are simply doing the best they can. If we can better equip a child's "toolbox," and be proactive with early support, rather than punish later behaviours, then we will start to see long lasting change.

Section 3 – A PSHE "Emotional Curriculum" and the "Five Core Competencies"

Having applied the PPT to individuals and groups of students we are now able to build up a picture of what the story behind their behaviour might be. We can look at this at an individual level and we can look at it at a school level. We can identify the different layers and we can consider what helps and what hinders. We must also return to my favourite quirky question: So, what?

I had an idea that there must be a set of skills or "core competencies" that were developmental and could be used with small groups of children and young people or full cohorts to support them along their journey. I came up with all sorts of variations before I remembered a colleague once telling me "the best ideas are always someone else's." With that in mind, I set about finding what was already out there. I came across an EEF guidance report from 2019, "Improving Social and Emotional Learning in Primary Schools" (van Poortvliet et al., 2021). There I found the five headings I was looking for:

- Self-awareness
- Self-management
- Social awareness
- Relationship skills
- Responsible decision making

These five headings became "core competencies" which perfectly framed exactly what I was thinking: We must support children in self-awareness. If they don't know who they are, they can't possibly think about anything or anyone else. Once they are self-aware, they can learn to self-manage. They must be supported in recognising and then managing their emotions and their behaviour. This is the essence of co-regulation and then self-regulation. When they are comfortable with these two competencies we can start to consider the wider circle of their social surroundings – the impact this has on them and the impact they have on it. The next step is to work on relationships and their accompanying skills before finally putting all this together so that we can make responsible decisions.

For the cohort profiled in section 2, the core competencies were delivered in one-hour weekly mentoring sessions over five half terms in groups of up to six children. The next step was to develop this into a "PSHE Emotional Curriculum." The last section of this chapter will provide a little more detail about the five core competencies and how schools might build programmes around them.

Core Competency 1 – Self-Awareness

Self-awareness is having the ability to recognise our emotions and thoughts and learning to understand how this influences our behaviour. Having self-awareness enables us to assess our strengths and recognise our limitations which in turn helps us develop a realistic view of what we are capable of. It gives us an appropriate confidence and optimism for the things we can do and helps us recognise and manage the things we can't. This equips us with accurate self-perception which means we can recognise who we actually are as opposed who or what we might pretend to be. It also helps to develop our self-efficacy (a belief in ourselves). Good self-awareness is associated with reduced difficulties in social functioning and fewer instances of externalising problems, in particular aggression.

This part of the "emotional curriculum" supports children with developing a knowledge of their emotions and increasing their ability to express them accurately. We can help children recognise and name their emotions through explicit teaching of "affect labelling" – putting feelings into words. We should provide activities that give children the opportunity to practise using this language in real contexts through games, stories, and role play.

Some examples of activities to develop self-awareness include:

- Using story books to discuss how characters feel and why they feel this way
- Using games to develop children's vocabulary, e.g. miming activities where children guess a feeling that is being portrayed ("emotional charades")
- Using mirrors, photographs, and pictures to talk about what happens to people's faces and bodies when they are experiencing particular emotions. For example, children might match photographs displaying different emotions with emotion labels and scenario labels
- Teaching them to use "I" messages, articulating how they feel and why: "I feel x because…"
- Using emotions posters alongside daily check-ins for children (further described in Chapter 7)
- Providing supportive prompts to children who have difficulty talking about their emotions such as: "It looks like you might be feeling sad, can you tell me what happened?" The simple act of naming the emotion can help children understand it more clearly
- Explaining to children that all feelings are okay, but the behaviours they lead to may not be okay. It is okay to feel angry, for example, but not okay to act in ways that hurt others

Core Competency 2 – Self-Management

Once we are aware of what makes us us, what specifically and uniquely gives us our multitude of emotions, we have to learn how to manage them. Self-management is the ability to successfully regulate our emotions, thoughts, and behaviours in different situations. This means we can effectively manage stress, control our impulses, and motivate ourselves. Self-management gives us the ability to set and work towards personal and academic goals.

The skills associated with self-management include impulse control, stress management, self-discipline, self-motivation, goal setting, and organisational skills. This also includes the ability to recognise, set, and maintain boundaries.

Self-management is important when we are frustrated, anxious, or excited and how we regulate following experiencing these emotions. It plays a key role in how we focus on a task and how we recognise and control our impulses and ultimately provides us with the ability to repair when things don't go to plan.

To help children and young people self-manage we need to develop their skills in taking turns, sharing, learning how to express their emotions appropriately, being more aware of their behaviour, understanding their emotions (what does impulse mean, how or why does that matter to me, what example do I have?), apologising, repeating and learning from challenges, humility, and understanding that it is okay to make a mistake.

Some examples of activities to develop self-management include:

- Counting to ten, walking away, telling someone how you feel, asking for help, knowing when to ask for help, accepting help
- Self-calming strategies (deep breathing, box breathing, tapping, butterfly hug – head down or hold self)
- Positive self-talk (being aware of negative automatic thinking styles, catastrophising, fortune telling, negative self-talk)
- Recognising body cues (early physiological signs such as the heart rate increasing, sweaty palms, tummy ache)
- Images or metaphors (volcano/balloon bursting/bottle exploding)

Core Competency 3 – Social Awareness

Once we have self-awareness and have learned how to recognise our triggers and manage our emotions, we must learn how what we do, and how we behave, impacts on those around us. Social awareness is our ability to take the perspective of and empathise with others. It is our ability to understand the social and ethical norms for behaviour and to recognise family, school, and community resources and supports. It means that we must not only understand our emotions but the feelings and emotions of others; we must begin to feel sympathy and empathy. It means we must learn to recognise and appreciate diversity and have respect for those we share the world with.

Children are naturally more ego-centric; they are more inclined to think about themselves and their own needs. Understanding the perspective of other people and developing empathy is fundamental for the positive development and mental health of children. Good social skills developed by ten years of age are predictors of a range of adult outcomes such as life satisfaction, labour market success, and good overall health.

The social norms our children are exposed to which they need help developing include manners; respect for self and others; social etiquette; family, school, and community rules; sharing; boundaries; personal space/touching; difference and diversity; humour; the ability to "let things go"; blame culture; honesty; and accepting responsibility.

Some examples of activities to develop self-management include:

- Practicing eating at a table
- Games which involve turn taking – this might start with a simple game passing a ball between two people
- Encouraging discussion about our day (this encourages them to talk and share their own experiences as well as taking turns in empathetically listening to others)

Core Competency 4 – Relationship Skills

Once we are aware of the people around us, we must learn how to interact with them positively and empathetically. Relationship skills provide us with the ability to establish and maintain healthy relationships with diverse individuals and groups. They help us to communicate clearly, listen well, cooperate with others, resist inappropriate social pressure, negotiate conflict constructively, and seek and offer help when needed. They enable us to effectively navigate social situations. It is important that children learn to recognise, express, and regulate their emotions before they can be expected to interact successfully with others.

Some examples of activities to build relationship skills include:

- Providing opportunities for reflection
- Modelling relationship building behaviour
- Peer mediation
- Group activities that require collaboration and teamwork
- Unstructured play with reflection time
- Role plays

- Circle time
- Discussion and collaboration with class rules

Core Competency 5 – Responsible Decision Making

Finally, once we have the skill set to build what are hopefully positive relationships, we must have the confidence and competence to make sensible decisions. Responsible decision making is our ability to make constructive choices about personal behaviour and social interactions. It gives us the ability to make a realistic evaluation of the consequences of our actions and allows us to take into consideration our own well-being and the well-being of others.

We need to help children to develop the skills and confidence they need to identify and address problems effectively. We must create a safe and supportive space where they feel comfortable expressing their thoughts and feelings without fear of judgement or punishment. We should avoid complex terminology and use simple, clear, and concrete language to help them understand and articulate their feelings and experiences. We should model active listening and reflect what we hear to validate their feelings, ensuring we understand their perspective. We should help the child express their feelings and identify problems in a non-threatening and enjoyable way. This can be achieved by using a step by step process to identify the problem, conceptualising possible solutions, evaluating the options, and then choosing the best solution. We should identify negative thought patterns and replace them with more positive and realistic thoughts.

To support children and young people when analysing solutions, we can do the following:

- When idea sharing, reinforce that there is no right or wrong
- Introduce critical thinking. What might happen if we try this solution? How would this make us and others feel? What are the good and bad things about this option? What can we learn from this?
- Roleplay to practise social skills in order to build confidence
- Encourage decision making
- Evaluate and reflect. After implementing the solution, discuss how it went. What worked well? What didn't? What could be done differently next time?

To encourage ethical responsibility, we must recognise that empathy is the corner stone of ethical behaviour. We should create age-appropriate ethical dilemmas and potential responses. Then we can encourage the children to think about the consequences of different actions. We should encourage reflective thinking, helping them to reflect on their actions and the potential impact this would have on others. We should ask questions like, "Can you put yourself in someone else's position and think how they might feel if …?" or "What do you think is the right thing to do and why?" We should discuss why core ethical values such as honesty, fairness, respect, responsibility, and kindness are important.

Reflection

- Do we have a forensic understanding of the story behind individual children's behaviour?
- Do we have a forensic understanding of the picture this creates across year groups and the whole school population?
- Do we have an emotional curriculum based on core competencies which has been designed to support the developmental journey of our children and young people?
- Is permanent exclusion ever the answer? Does it solve a problem or create a problem? If not permanent exclusion, then what?

This chapter re-affirms the thinking behind the first guiding principle – if a child could do better, then they would. The Pupil Profile Tool helps us build up a picture to understand why children might react the way they do and provides alternative strategies to help them and us recognise and remember that all emotions are okay whilst understanding that the way their emotions affect their behaviour can impact others negatively.

The emotional curriculum and core competencies look at what makes us human. This is not a learning to learn curriculum, as before children can learn we must consider how their brains work and what makes them tick. By looking closely at how children and young people are responding to what is around them it helps us recognise the sequence of their developing brains. The PPT and core competencies can help us identify and then address the survival mechanisms that might have developed differently because of a lack of safety. The core competency emotional curriculum also helps to provide alternative ways of behaving in the environments inhabited outside school. It provides an opportunity for our internal blueprints to further readjust to make sense of the world we inhabit.

If the world our children and young people inhabit is dangerous or lacks love, their internal maps may develop to reflect their version of reality. This doesn't always provide an accurate picture of what the world is like or how the world works, and this can be really confusing for children and young people. We may not be able to change their world outside school, but we can offer alternatives and plant seeds which may develop and grow further down the line.

Some children have begun to develop what might be considered a faulty narrative, a narrative which serves to protect them from harm but by doing so can distort healthy development. With co-regulated support, gentle nudges, time, and explanation, they can be supported in rewriting their narrative. The corrective red pen and red lines of punitive discipline only serve to distance the children further from the safe world they deserve and are entitled to live in. Teaching an emotional curriculum through the core competencies supports children in recognising the choices they make and the impact this might have on themselves and others whilst equipping them with the tools to manage difficult situations. Ultimately this will reduce instances of dysregulated behaviour, avoiding shame and blame.

References

Burke, Harris, N. (2018). *The deepest well*. Bluebird.

Pedersen, T. (2022, July 8). *All about somatic anxiety*. PsychCentral. https://psychcentral.com/anxiety/somatic-anxiety?scrlybrkr=37efe58e

van Poortvliet M., Clarke, A. & Gross, Jean. (2021, October 27). *Improving social and emotional learning in primary schools – guidance report*. The Education Endowment Foundation (EEF). https://d2tic4wvo1iusb.cloudfront.net/production/eef-guidance-reports/primary-sel/EEF_Social_and_Emotional_Learning.pdf?v=1722873666

Perry, B. & Winfrey, O. (2021). *What happened to you? Conversations on trauma, resilience, and healing*. Bluebird.

Chapter 6
Words

For all of us who work in education, we cannot escape from the power of words and the importance of thoughtful communication. The words we use in our schools impact on so many stakeholders that we would be foolish to not think carefully about what we say and how we say it. After all, "Words are seeds that do more than blow around. They land in our hearts and not the ground. Be careful what you plant and careful what you say. You might have to eat what you planted one day" (anonymous author).

This chapter will focus on how we consciously craft our words to support a Relationally Inclusive approach and specifically look at our five key vocabularies; it will identify and explain some *need-to-know* trauma and attachment specific phrases; and it will look at how some schools (and maybe society in general) have slipped into using language which criminalises children.

***

If Dr Bruce Lipton is correct in saying, "Our words reflect our state of mind and our expectations of the world," then we must think very carefully about the words we use to support the practice of *Relational Inclusion*. It is probably therefore necessary to explore the reasoning behind calling this *Relational Inclusion* in the first place.

I never set out with the intention of creating something new and original. Nor would I claim that this is new and original. There is so much out there and so many different interpretations of very similar things yet equally I couldn't find anything that quite did what I was trying to do in terms of improving my school.

What I did learn very quickly was that using terms like "trauma" and "attachment" becomes very complicated in a school environment. For a

DOI: 10.4324/9781003532866-7

start there is an aspect of technical language which comes straight from the semantic field of psychology, therapy, and counselling. The vast majority of staff who work in schools aren't psychologists, therapists, or counsellors and don't need to be. However as soon as you present to teachers and school staff and use this language, you unintentionally distance yourself from them. Whether true or not, generally therapists aren't teachers or support staff or school leaders and vice-versa.

Secondly, the research underpinning some of the theory is changing quickly as neuroscience develops. This is no bad thing, but if you pin your practice to a specific theory and that theory changes, from a school perspective, you can end up in an awkward predicament.

Finally, as a school leader, I have never been interested in achieving a "badge" or a "gold mark" that celebrates my commitment to a particular practice. This is no criticism of anyone who chooses such a path. The risk is you end up committing too much time to passing certain elements to achieve certain awards and whilst that is happening it is possible that you might just take your eye of the core purpose: Improving the lives and chances of the children and communities we serve.

I looked for something which represented what it said on the tin. You cannot work in education (or exist in the world) and not recognise the importance of relationships. As a result of that, the word "relational" seemed to make sense. It must be at the heart of everything we do.

I also think that schools must be inclusive. I acknowledge that the practice and even a true definition of inclusion has become murky. However, true inclusion must become a non-negotiable. These are all *our* children; we must share the responsibility we have for them. Exclusion of any kind must be recognised for what it is. We must no longer hide behind phrases like "we are doing this for their own good" or "they will be better in a different environment." For me, these are at best an example of a naïve misunderstanding that others can do what you can't and at worst a euphemism better expressed with the more honest statement of "these are difficult children who we don't feel we can manage anymore." I am not saying that there aren't really good "alternative" provisions and special schools out there. I am saying that in my experience there are some children that some mainstream schools just don't want. I am really saddened that I have had to write that line. And maybe that is why I decided *Relational* and *Inclusion* are exactly the two words, together, which represent everything I am trying to do.

Five Key Vocabularies

The guiding principles were written to help us understand what *Relational Inclusion* "feels" like in a school. How a school feels provides clear insight into its culture and ethos. Schools are noisy places; what should *Relational Inclusion* "sound" like? Words are so important and the wrong use of words at the wrong time can cause a great deal of damage and harm. Initially I explored the deliberate use of five words, and these became the **Five Key Vocabularies** which all the schools using Relational Inclusion as an approach have adopted. The first word is possibly the most important of them all.

1. Dysregulation

I have spent three-quarters of my career wrongly describing and naming difficult and challenging incidents. I suppose this is unsurprising as it is exactly these events which trigger an emotional response; they set our nervous system racing and when the amygdala takes over, as I have described in previous chapters, survival mode kicks in and I guess an adrenalin-driven hypervigilant state is accompanied with its own very specific vocabulary.

This is obviously not unique to life in school; in fact I could argue it is events and normalised fight or flight responses in the community and on the world stage which drive a hostile linguistic response. I spent the best part of 20 years describing students (and staff) as having "kicked off" or "ballooned" or "tantrummed" or "lost it." To be fair, I was only describing what I thought I was seeing. But ignorance is no excuse. For this kind of language sits alongside shaming practice and humiliation. It emphasises the individual first as opposed to defining what they are experiencing. In Relational Inclusion we use the word **dysregulated** to describe any instance where a child or member of staff is struggling.

To illustrate why this is important, let's consider things which aren't associated with so-called "naughty children." For example, instead of calling someone an obese person or an alcoholic, we should reframe this to reflect their condition. It would be more accurate to say that they suffer with alcoholism or from obesity. Here we are taking the blame away from the person and recognising that they are struggling with a medical condition. This is often referred to as "person-first language" or "person-centred language."

Reframing is part of a broader movement to reduce stigma and promote empathy and understanding towards individuals with various conditions. It reflects an understanding that behaviours and conditions often stem from underlying health issues rather than personal failings or moral shortcomings.

The thinking behind this approach is rooted in several principles:

1. **Humanisation**: Recognizing the person as more than their condition
2. **Empathy**: Encouraging a compassionate understanding of the challenges they face
3. **Reducing stigma**: Mitigating negative stereotypes and discrimination associated with certain conditions
4. **Promoting dignity**: Respecting the inherent dignity and worth of all individuals

(ChatGPT)

In *Relational Inclusion*, we define dysregulation as being

> when a person is in crisis and is struggling to manage their emotions. Emotional dysregulation is a poor ability to manage emotional responses or keep them within an acceptable range of typical emotional reactions (e.g. sadness, anger, irritability, and frustration).

We invest in training our staff and our young people in recognising and understanding when a person is dysregulated, and we deliberately and consciously use this word and remind and correct ourselves and others should we slip back into our old habits of careless language.

2. Co-regulation

Once a school has begun to establish a culture and ethos which understands and recognises as a community the signs and symptoms of dysregulated behaviour we must return to the *so what* question. How do we help someone who is dysregulated? I suppose the answer is glaringly obvious: They need support to become regulated. Initially this is a difficult thing to achieve on your own. If you think back to previous chapters of this book and, indeed, one of its key themes, I have talked a lot about relationships. This is where "co-regulation" comes into play.

In *Relational Inclusion*, we define co-regulation as being

when another person helps a child who is dysregulated to manage their emotions. This is achieved through warm and responsive interactions that provide the support, coaching, and modelling children need to understand, express, and modulate their thoughts, feelings, and behaviours.

The definition above specifies "children"; however this approach also applies to dysregulated members of staff and even parents or carers. Schools who are really proficient in using these strategies are also able to train their children and young people in co-regulation strategies so that they too can support other dysregulated children where and when this is appropriate.

3. Self-regulation

For all of us who have worked with children, it seems natural (at least to me) that we spend a lot of time thinking about the children we have failed. It seems to be a core part of working in schools for some reason. For me, in particular, there have been several children who had such difficult personal backgrounds that, although I (and many other staff) managed to make school something of a safe place for them, they fell into significant difficulties quite quickly after leaving. It is those children I think of now. I truly believe that if we had used the steps discussed in this book, we might well have managed to help them live better lives.

If we can recognise when we are dysregulated, if we have the support of an adult or a friend who can help us co-regulate, with time and practice, we can apply some of these strategies and techniques and learn to self-regulate. If we can do this, if our young people can do this, we just might start to make different decisions and choices at key points in our lives, which might be transformational.

In *Relational Inclusion* we define self-regulation as being "when a student (or adult) can manage their own emotional responses. This is achieved by conscious personal management allowing an individual to guide and manage their own thoughts, behaviours, and feelings."

4. Window of tolerance

I think an understanding of my own *window of tolerance* has been one of the biggest lightbulb moments for me as I've travelled down the trauma and attachment rabbit hole. Slightly embarrassingly, I think I sort of used to believe in omens. Let me explain. If, when I woke up, one or two things "went wrong" before I left the house, I used to see this as an omen. I used to brace myself for a "bad day." Somehow, *I* "knew" that the way the day had started meant I had to watch my step and check my temper because "it was going to be one of those days."

I wasn't catastrophising and I wasn't really creating a self-fulfilling prophecy. I just didn't know I had a window of tolerance and that on such days, a small list of things "going wrong" was simply narrowing my "window of tolerance" and ultimately affecting my mood. By not recognising this, it began to impact on my day ahead as generally I got grumpier and grumpier (which is something of an understatement). My closest friends have commented that I have mellowed in my "old age," but this is my secret: I just learned to recognise, better understand, and manage my "window of tolerance."

In *Relational Inclusion* we define window of tolerance as "the zone in which a person can function most effectively. It is the place where intense emotional arousal can be processed in a healthy way allowing you to function and react to stress or anxiety effectively."

5. Attachment (or connection) seeking

I have taught so many children who were so desperate for attention. It seems such a shame that often in society we view this negatively. The phrase "attention seeking" has connotations rooted in shame and humiliation but once we begin to see these children through an attachment lens, everything changes. After all, if we give them the attention they so desperately seek; if we see this as attachment and connection; if we do this consistently and in the right way, then children will no longer have to seek what they should have and are entitled to anyway.

In *Relational Inclusion* "we use attachment (or connection) seeking as opposed to attention seeking. We understand that often anxious students need a secure base because of on/off parenting. They use over developed verbal skills to gain reassurance."

Language Used to Criminalise Children

One of the things you learn to do as a senior leader is walk around your school and listen. Unfortunately, the longer you spend at a particular school the less you hear. More specifically, you start to hear and notice the things that you and your leadership team are focusing on and become deaf and blind to some of the more obvious things which can sometimes be more important and pressing. This, I suppose, is just a consequence of becoming institutionalised, but this cannot be used as an excuse. Like everything else, we need to practise listening consciously and carefully. Sometimes we need to invite other leaders in to listen (and go and listen for them) as they will certainly hear the things we miss.

For Relational Inclusion, I have spent a lot of time listening to and thinking about some of the everyday language we use in schools around managing children's behaviour. I have needed to reflect on my own practice and ideology as I have used, believed, and validated all the words and phrases I will discuss below. In fact, if, four years ago, you told me what I am about to explain, I would have replied that it's claptrap; that it's idealistic nonsense. I would have described very successful "outstanding" schools who swear the opposite and, on the surface, have the results to back up such a claim. Somehow over the years, criminal language has slipped into everyday use, so much so that we don't even notice. Once you do notice, it is hard not to tug at the thread. It takes a lot of time and effort to unwind misconceptions that are so heavily imbedded and ingrained into everyday practice. But if we are to do our children and our communities justice, this is something we must explore.

According to Dr Rick Hanson (2013), our brains have a natural "negativity bias which makes it like Velcro for the bad and Teflon for the good. So, we must learn to take in the positive experiences, weaving them into the fabric of our brains." By using the language of the courts in our schools we are starting from a negative mindset. For example, a behaviour policy implies that children won't behave and provides the consequences of what then happens. (If you look at the majority of school behaviour policy there is far more time given to consequences than rewards.) When a child dysregulates in school, we often refer to the situation as an "incident" rather than recognising this isn't necessarily a choice. This instantly shifts our state of mind, creating a negative perception of the child. In turn the child sees they are being judged critically by staff or other children and begin to perceive themselves negatively. This then becomes a self-fulfilling prophecy where children begin to live up to negative expectations. It is necessary therefore to rewrite some of the narrative used in schools, to think carefully about the language we use and begin from a positive starting point.

Using criminalising language for children oversimplifies and masks complex issues. Let's take a look at some of the common language we use which criminalises children and explore how we could use words differently.

Incident and Offence

When a child "behaves badly" and this escalates, we tend to describe the event as an **incident** and the misbehaviour as an **offence**. This is a massive oversimplification of a complex situation as stated above. The word "incident" suggests that a "single thing" has happened, and therefore someone is to blame. The fact that we refer to "the thing" that has happened as an **offence** implies conscious choice, criminality, and therefore punishment. None of this language or associated thinking considers ACEs, trauma, attachment, and all the aspects of Relational Inclusion that this book details. Most importantly it doesn't consider the fact that the child themselves may be hurting. If we adopt a child-centred approach and look carefully for the "cause and not the symptoms," often the escalation can be prevented and the dysregulation can become a learning opportunity enabling the child to grow.

Assault, Criminal Damage, and Vandalising

I have selected three examples from a long list of perceived offences. Let's start with assault. Without describing the details of a perceived assault, inevitably a member of staff tells me that a child has assaulted another child or indeed a member of staff. Using the term **assault** is emotive and unhelpful.

The definition of assault in legal terms is:

> a tort and criminal offence that occurs when a person intentionally or recklessly causes another person to apprehend the infliction of immediate and unlawful force on their body.
>
> (CPS, 2024)

The issue with using this phrase in schools is that assault is a judgement. This tells us nothing about the event that has happened. It also implies that the child has done whatever they have done deliberately with the intention of hurting someone else. I have been told that children as young as five have "assaulted" other children or staff. The connotations of assault are that there should follow a serious consequence or punishment. Surely, we should be working with children to develop co- and self-regulation as opposed to naming a behaviour to justify a punishment.

The same could be said for the terms **criminal damage** and **vandalism**. How can we begin to understand what has happened or why it has happened and find a solution if we don't know the detail and are simply making judgements?

When children damage property, it tends to be as a result of a surge of emotions. They are operating from fight or flight and their amygdala is managing their behaviour. I am not excusing kicking walls or doors. I am simply advocating that responding to the symptom is ineffective and doesn't address or change long-term behaviour.

Here we could take a note out of the safeguarding guidance. Information should be non-judgemental and factual.

Feral, Repeat Offender, Chosen Behaviour

Dysregulated children are often referred to as **feral**, they are labelled as **repeat offenders**, and this is justified by schools as being the child's **chosen behaviour**. It feels almost ridiculous to explain these terms now I have written them down. They are all born from a blame and shame system. **Feral** comes from the use of a deficit narrative (as described in Chapter 5). Children are not feral. They are surviving the best way that they can. They may need support, guidance, and patience but surely comparing them to Romulus and Remus is entirely inappropriate.

Equally labelling them as **repeat offenders** highlights a school's inability or unwillingness to meet need. If our children keep making the same mistakes, doesn't that reflect our failings? Isn't it our job to recognise that something isn't working and try a different approach as opposed to ultimately blaming the child because our methods are ineffective? As Einstein supposedly said, "the definition of insanity is doing the same thing over and over and expecting a different result."

I have heard too many school leaders explain that the child has purposely done whatever they have done, that it is their **chosen behaviour** and therefore they need punishing. The neuroscience discussed in this book highlights that there is often very little conscious choice behind some of the behaviours our children demonstrate. We need to support, recognise, and understand before guiding, modelling, and supporting positive change.

Zero Tolerance, Policing the School, and Walkie-Talkies

I have referred to zero-tolerance approaches used by schools throughout the book and am not about to labour the same points here. I would just like to draw attention to the very words themselves. In a school community what do they even mean? We are dealing with children and young people, some of whom come from unstable home backgrounds. What exactly are we applying zero tolerance to? In schools we do not represent or work for the country's legal system. We are not the judge and the jury. Are we actually advocating for and justifying, in words, a set of black and white rules about the grey area of "behaviour"? Behaviour which can be labelled and tariffed arbitrarily depending on an individual's whim of what is deemed right and wrong, whilst at the same time choosing to ignore the neuroscientific research about how the brain works and adapts depending on a child's individual circumstances and need. Even within our legal system, mitigation is considered. It is also important to remember that these children must go somewhere. What would happen to them if all schools and PRUs adopted a zero-tolerance approach? Where would they go? Who would be responsible and accountable for them? Or is the PRU to prison pipeline a term and reality that we are happy and comfortable with?

With hard and fast rules comes a system of reinforcement. Some leadership or pastoral teams find themselves quite literally **policing the school**. They have "patrols," and "duty points" and "hotspots" and "blind spots." Please don't confuse what I am saying with the safeguarding needs of a school. Of course, our children and young people must be kept safe. Of course, there must be close supervision. Must we shine our boots and march the corridors to achieve this?

A pet hate of mine (and again I was once an advocate of this) is the wonderful walkie-talkie. Apart from the issues we faced in one school over the fact that people outside school could tune into the same wavelength and hear exactly what was being said leading to all sorts of potential safeguarding issues, wouldn't it be an interesting exercise to transcribe the walkie-talkie conversations. What on earth are we doing and why?

Equally I've worked in schools where something has happened, a child is hypervigilant but beginning to regulate, and then a radio crackles, and a member of staff clumsily recounts the event emotively in full hearing range of the child causing further escalation and tension. I have also worked in schools where there are different codes for different events. The children take great delight in breaking the codes and besides, the clear panic in the radio announcer's pitch often means that no code is necessary anyway. My point here is that a walkie-talkie can simply become an extension of a police-based victim and criminal method of managing crime and we work in schools. We don't need to **police our schools**; we need to care for our children and avoid creating fever pitch environments which further escalate the behaviours and emotions we are trying to prevent.

Witness Statement

When a problematic event has occurred in school, for some reason we have adopted the practice of taking **witness statements**. These are problematic for many reasons. First of all, those of us working in schools are not the police. Secondly witnesses are fairly unreliable at the best of times and this is heightened when children are asked to recount events and friends or hidden agendas maybe involved. Regardless of the biases we or the children might apply, we must also remember that "we don't respond to what happens, we respond to our perception of what happens" (Mate, 2019) and watching any Derren Brown show will highlight how unreliable our ability to recall events accurately is.

Although all the above points are relevant, they also demonstrate how far we have become removed from our actual purpose. You see, taking a **witness statement** presumes a **crime**. Along with a **crime** there must be a **target** or a **victim**. For this to be the case there must be a **perpetrator**. And once all the mess has occurred, there must be a fitting **punishment**. Are we not focusing on totally the wrong thing? I think Terry Pratchett may well have described this as "going down the wrong trouser leg" (Pratchett, 1989). It took a conversation with Dr Luke Roberts to clarify this for me. He said there "is the tendency for schools to focus on what they **don't** want rather than what they **do** want" (Roberts, 2024). Initially I didn't understand but I think **witness statements** illustrate this point beautifully.

You see **witness statements** are a result of thinking about what we don't want in schools. We don't want bad behaviour and all the paragraphs above are a response to what happens and what we do when this occurs. If we were to flip this and think about what we do want, we might say we want harmony and understanding with the ability to repair any conflict. To achieve these goals, we would have to consider the event through a totally different lens.

The outcome of any incident would be less significant than the steps which led up to it and possibly the circumstances which created the dysregulation so that we could pre-empt and prevent or support such dysregulation before it escalated further.

Isolation

I've mentioned previously the ineffective nature of detentions as a consequence in schools. When a child "fails" detention or their behaviour is seen as more serious (not more complex), they often find themselves in isolation. And don't get me wrong. I was once an advocate of isolation and its accompanying booths. I was recently in a meeting and the school referred to the booths as "high-sided desks." Semantics are wonderful things.

Again, let us put this in perspective. When a prisoner is a danger to themselves and or others, they may be isolated or placed in solitary confinement. Even for prisoners, this can be very damaging for their mental health. But we aren't dealing with prisoners in schools, we're dealing with children and young people. At what point did we decided that children who couldn't manage sitting quietly in detention for an hour; that children who struggle to sit still anyway; that children who have made some infringement of school rules, which might only be wearing the wrong shoes or having the wrong hair style or missing multiple homeworks, would have their needs better met or be supported into making "better choices next time" by being isolated for at least a day? And in many cases, it's a week or longer.

Let's be clear what isolation rooms try to enforce: Sitting silently, facing a wall; ideally (if some schools have their way) not even being able to see another person and working.

And let's clarify what "working" means. At best the subject teacher has a few minutes to explain an hour's learning. At worst death by worksheet or copying something out.

So, it's possible that we have somehow decided that it's okay (in fact it's accepted as a right) to take what are often some of our most troubled children who are suffering from ACEs or trauma or attachment and place them in isolation.

Many of these children are already behind with their learning. It would even be fair to argue that their low levels of literacy are the conduit to some of their behaviours in the first place. So is it really a good idea to remove them from even more of their learning? I hear the counter argument: But they are stopping others from learning. If this is the case, who is taking the time to think curiously about why this might be the case? Could it be that these children actually need more intensive support?

Imagine if the small group of isolated children actually became a small group with a Relationally Inclusive support package (you might want to read Chapter 5 again). Is it possible that this might begin to break the cycle?

Surely, it's time for schools to reconsider their use of isolation rooms, isolation booths, and high sided desks. We also know that there is a disproportionate use of these facilities with children who have special educational needs. To make matters worse, if that is possible, there is no evidence that this approach works. Whilst schools may argue that the rest of the class can learn without interruption, they fail to demonstrate how isolation has been beneficial for the child struggling with dysregulation.

When did we allow schools to prioritise the majority at the expense of a small number of children? Is this the kind of society we want to promote?

How on earth are these issues overlooked by education's watchdog, Ofsted?

Whilst it is also true that there are situations where it is not beneficial for a child struggling to regulate their behaviour to remain in class, surely our most vulnerable children deserve respect and should be allowed to address their issues with well-trained staff in a private setting away from their peers.

Reflection

- Are we confident using the five key vocabularies?
- Do we recognise when and where we are using criminalising language with children and why this is unhelpful?
- Are we curious enough about how and why children behave the way that they do to a point that we have a desire to change the language we use?

If we stop

- Seeing children's behaviour through the criminal lens of incident and offence
- Labelling our children as feral or repeat offenders or describing their behaviour as chosen
- Using zero-tolerance approaches and "policing" our schools

- Taking witness statements and issuing tariff-based punishments
- Using isolation rooms and booths as behaviour correction or modification tools

Then we might start:

- Seeing the child who sits behind the behaviour
- Accepting that some children are trying to indicate and communicate that things are not okay with a vocabulary they don't yet (and possibly shouldn't ever) have because the emotions they are feeling are the result of events outside of their control
- Accepting that they are just children

As I write, the most common reason given for permanent exclusion in schools in the United Kingdom is persistent disruptive behaviour. Imagine if this was rephrased as consistent emotional dysregulation.

Would that be a good enough reason to permanently exclude some of the nation's most vulnerable children?

References

CPS. (2024, July 23). *Offences against the person, incorporating the charging standard.* https://www.cps.gov.uk/legal-guidance/offences-against-person-incorporating-charging-standard

Hanson., R. (2013). *Hardwiring happiness: The new brain science of contentment, calm, and confidence.* Harmony Books.

Mate, G. (2019). *When the body says no: The cost of hidden stress.* Vermilion.

Pratchett, T. (1989). *Wyrd sisters.* Transworld Publishers Ltd.

Roberts, L. (2024). *Leading schools and sustaining innovation.* Routledge.

Chapter 7

Fostering a Culture of Compassion

I hope that by this point in the book, you recognise and agree with the importance of prioritising relationships, especially with our children and young people, and in doing everything in our power to support the most educationally inclusive practice possible. It is our duty to understand the influence we have on how our children develop and how, in turn, they will shape the very fabric of the future. As Nelson Mandela (1995) said, "There can be no keener revelation of a society's soul than the way in which it treats its children." It is therefore necessary to re-examine the foundation of our schools' systems and approaches to behaviour. Fostering understanding, empathy, and support is the most effective way to nurture our children and build a sustainable and more satisfied society. Chapter 7 will discuss how *Relational Inclusion* helps creates a sense of belonging and compassion; why we need to understand how confusing the multiple rule-based worlds our children inhabit are; and how helping children to repair their mistakes prevents lasting shame and further trauma.

Our children can only inherit what we leave behind for them. Do we want our legacy to be one of fear and worry or hope and compassion?

***

Part 1 – The Problem with Compliance

There are many times in the life of a teacher when we suffer from self-doubt or question our ability to do the job. The responsibility for raising and guiding future generations is enormous and if we don't feel the weight of that duty then we are probably in the wrong profession. As mentioned on several occasions throughout the book, the mindset of the teacher is fundamental in the success or failure of any behaviour system or relational approach. Addressing misbehaviour promptly, thoughtfully, and consistently is essential, not only to prevent escalation and feelings of shame but also to promote healing and growth.

What exactly are the issues with a compliance-based behaviour approach? Why doesn't punitive punishment work? Why are detention halls filled with the same children night after night? Why are more and more children being suspended and permanently excluded? Surely, if a compliance-based system and approach worked, then by now, all the children would be behaving themselves and poor behaviour would have been eradicated from schools.

I think it's important to start by thinking about what it is we actually want from the children and young people who sit in front of us. Do we want them to obey unquestioningly, or do we want them to comply and conform because they know and understand it is the right thing to do?

A discipline model, where there are clear and rigid tariffs for specific behaviours, over-activates the fear system and children move into fight or flight (as discussed in Chapter 2). This means that although initially children may comply (and it is possibly this "quick win" that has sustained the misguided belief that such a system works in schools), it

> quickly moves our traumatised pupils into difficult states like fear and terror. Fear driven compliance may suit us in the short term but can have negative long-term consequences for the child's welfare, functioning and life and the community at large, later on.
> (Bombèr, 2020)

It also means that whilst we may get compliance, this is "only because the child is frightened of us or the trouble they will be in if they don't comply" (Phillips et al., 2020). This means that our children, who often can't control some of their behavioural responses, which happen because their nervous system is trying to protect them, also aren't learning about how and why they should behave in a particular way or situation. They don't learn how to calm their nervous system, so they repeat the same patterns, and their behaviours don't change.

With a punitive behaviour approach, when behaviour doesn't improve, the tendency is to ramp up the consequences. In essence we are backing the children into a corner and offering them no chance of escape whilst simultaneously continuing to threaten their nervous system, increasing the chances of further dysregulated and threatening behaviour. We are poking the bear and then wondering why it roars, rears up on its hind legs, and attacks.

I used the analogy of a factory earlier in the book. Unlike "a production line, education requires constant adaptation. The very institutions designed to promote learning no longer learn themselves" (Roberts, 2024). As discussed in Chapter 1, the basic idea behind compliance behaviour models hasn't changed very much since the Victorian days. The difference is that we do now understand a little bit more about how the brain and nervous system works and so we must apply this new learning in our schools.

To foster a culture of compassion we must first have a shared understanding of what happens in the brain when children dysregulate. The first step is to correct our language as described in Chapter 6. It is still very easy to slip into using terms like "when children don't behave." However, words like this suggest their behaviour is "chosen." If we support staff and children to understand how the brain and nervous system work and how this may affect our choices and "behaviour" then we can adapt the way we manage these situations. The "Hand Model of the Brain" is one such strategy.

The Hand Model of the Brain

A really simple way to understand what is going on when dysregulation occurs is called the *"Hand Model of the Brain,"* a concept created by Dr Dan Siegel. If you hold up your hand so that your palm faces you and your fingers are resting together, we have a very basic version of the brain.

The line in the heel of your hand, where your hand joins your wrist, represents your brain stem. This part of the brain controls basic bodily functions that we need to survive such as regulating your heartbeat, breathing, body temperature, and balance.

If you now fold your thumb across your palm (as though resting your thumb tip at the base of your little finger), this represents your amygdala. This is an almond-shaped structure and although it is small, it plays a big part in your emotional responses. This is the part of the brain that responds and has quite a lot of control when we are in "fight" or "flight" mode.

Finally, if you fold your fingers over your thumb and almost hold your hand as though it were a puppet, you can see the brain shape as it fits inside your head. Your folded fingers represent your pre-frontal cortex. This is often referred to as the thinking brain. This is the part of the brain that puts us in that *sweet spot* for learning. If our pre-frontal cortex is on-line, it generally means we are calm and receptive, we are in a state of social engagement.

The Hand Model of the Brain is really useful for staff and children and young people. This shouldn't be kept as a secret; it isn't a magical tool to be used for control and power.

Flipping the Lid

This model also helps us to understand what happens when we go into fight or flight. Dan Siegal calls this *"flipping the lid."* To demonstrate, all you need to do is flip your four fingers up so that they no longer cover your thumb. If you remind yourself of the stress response list in Chapter 5, this is our nervous system response when we are threatened. This could be in response to a loud crash or bang; to someone cutting us up on the motorway; to someone shouting at us or telling us off. It is that all too familiar feeling of our cheeks flushing, our mouth going dry, and time seeming to slow right down. When this happens, we have *"flipped our lids."* Our pre-frontal cortex gives way to our amygdala to help us get back to safety.

The problem arises when we encounter someone who has *"flipped their lid"* but either don't recognise it, ignore it, or we have "flipped our own lids." Whilst we are operating largely through our amygdala, we are not capable of making rational, calm, and sensible choices. Nor are we able to hear practical recommendations when suggested by someone else. We will not be open to learning Shakespearian quotes or algebraic formulas. Our brains are simply in the wrong state to process this kind of information or learning.

Typically, when an adult meets a child in this state, we fire questions and facts at them, and we raise our voices. All of these actions add fuel to the fire of someone whose nervous system is trying to defend itself. What we actually need to do is bring the pre-frontal cortex back online. After all, "you can't teach someone to swim when they are drowning" (attributed to Milton Friedman).

Now that we understand some of the story behind the behaviour, what can we do differently? How can we apply compassion? Some useful strategies for co-regulation which calm the amygdala include the following.

Talking with Empathy

TISUK recommend using the acronym WINE (Trauma Informed Schools UK) (I **W**onder ... I **I**magine ... I **N**otice ... with **E**mpathy). This is an effective method for remembering how to start sentences when engaging with someone who has dysregulated. If, for example, a child is clenching and unclenching their fists, we might begin a conversation the following way:

> "I **notice** you are clenching your fist. I **wonder** if you are feeling really cross and frustrated and I **imagine** that you are finding it a little difficult to concentrate right now." (There is no need to use all the **WINE** verbs in every exchange! I just wanted to demonstrate how it could be used.)

Initially, it feels a bit awkward to talk in this way but with a little bit of practice you will be surprised how effective it can be. It is also important to allow the person you are co-regulating to correct you if you are wrong. They may well say that this is not the case and that they are feeling something different. The importance is "talking with empathy" as opposed to being right. This allows them to feel seen and heard and in turn this starts to enable the pre-frontal cortex to operate again.

"Talking with empathy" should not be confused with positive framing. I worked with a secondary school and the headteacher explained how they had already started to use a different approach where they "positively framed" their sentences. For example, a teacher might say, "Thank you for putting your pens down and listening carefully." As opposed to, "Put your pens down, shut up and listen." With positive framing we assume the best about students and narrate the positives. Positive framing does not address how responses might be affected by the nervous system. This is a very different approach to "talking with empathy."

Mental State Talk

When we are worried about something, we often feel it first. Often this is a sense of unease or an ache in our stomach (that's the vagus nerve again) (see Chapter 4). When children feel unsafe, their nervous system responds. They don't know why they feel how they do and often they don't have the vocabulary to describe their emotions. Without words they can be left with little option but to "behave their feelings" and "anger is sometimes fear's bodyguard" (Desautels, 2020). Feelings and emotions can be very confusing for all of us: "Sadness often looks like anger and fear can look like sadness. Anger is often actually fear, terror or sadness" (de Thierry, 2019).

Interestingly "our repertoire of words for calling people names is often larger than our vocabulary of words to clearly describe our emotional states" (Kahneman, 2011). Mental state talk or affect labelling is a way of helping young people to put words to their feelings. It's a simple concept really: Talking about our feelings can make us feel better. Providing rich vocabulary and recognizing, naming, and accepting all emotions without judgement can really support co-regulation. As Dan Siegal & Tina Payne Bryson (2011) says, "If you can name it, you can tame it."

Attunement

Attunement is our ability to respond to the emotions a child is displaying. For example, if you are really furious, if you have "flipped your lid" and steam is spouting from your ears, the last thing you need is someone gently suggesting you calm down. I can only speak for myself here, but never mind "flipping my lid," tell me to calm down when I'm fuming and I'm more than likely to "blow my top."

With attunement, we attune to the pain. We should try to meet the student at about a third of their emotional state. By "meeting the energy of the child's distress" (Trauma Informed Schools UK, n.d.), the child feels seen and heard and the amygdala can begin to take a backward step in its control over the fight or flight responses.

Check-in for Children

A daily check-in for children (as opposed to staff as described in Chapter 5) allows them to talk about how they are feeling in a safe and structured way. It follows exactly the same pattern as the staff check-in and it develops co-regulation as a daily habit, helping to ready them for a day of learning. You know what they say about a problem shared… We also use the daily check-in to teach children short mindfulness techniques that can help them to deal with stress and to self-regulate. Where children are suffering from trauma or toxic stress then they can be directed to specialists, in the pastoral team, who have the time and skills to help them to recover.

Part 2 – Restorative Practice

Another way to build compassion in schools is to understand and embed restorative conversations. Unfortunately, this is more complicated than it seems. When I began my journey down the rabbit hole of trauma informed practice, one of the first tunnels I explored was restorative practice. Very quickly I ran into several dead ends. There are plenty of scripts describing how to carry out restorative conversations. They usually involve a meeting between the child, adult, and possibly a third party. They take place in a neutral space after the event. Then a scripted conversation is used to explore feelings on both sides and hopefully resolve the conflict. The issue for me was that a script just didn't work. Apart from anything else, children could see through the script and the process seemed disingenuous. Schools went through the motions, ticked the restorative box, and nothing really changed. Restorative practice became a synonym for a short detention accompanied by a discussion which had to take place before the staff member and child could go home. Often the idea of restorative practice is translated into a script of five questions which are laminated onto paper the size of a credit card and attached to a lanyard. This quite literal reduction signifies how process can quickly replace the value, understanding, and significance of the underlying theory.

The dumbing down of theory leads to a lack of understanding. Often training is limited, oversimplified, or brushed over and this leads to many staff being reluctant or unable to engage with a truly restorative process. Without the proper training, restorative practice can become stressful for staff and children. Staff may be worried about making the situation worse. When dealing with very complex children, the member of staff may be reluctant to invest the time in what could feel like a very unsupportive, emotional, and challenging process.

Sometimes the member of staff has simply gone through the process of self-reflection on their own, recognised the part they played, realised the position the child was in, found their own "emotional peace," and "moved on." It is then incredibly difficult for them to revisit a thought process which they have managed internally. The problem here is that no-one has helped the child to benefit from exploring and experiencing the process of repair.

It is important for schools to establish a process where staff understand that restorative conversations are not just about an individual returning to their place of comfort, but also about the child's learning and growth. If the harm inflicted is not addressed, the child misses a vital learning opportunity. The child may feel regret and shame over their actions, but without discussion, these feelings can be buried deep inside. The child's internal working model may then adapt, encouraging them to believe that such incidents can be ignored and that repairing relationships is unimportant. Addressing the impact of our actions helps us to restore harmony, build relationships, and foster a culture of trust and respect. Most teachers have been in situations where they dread or fear the next lesson because of an unresolved issue or tension. Children also experience this and if we don't support young people by providing them with strategies for repair, this can lead to further dysregulation. Without the opportunity for repair, we create a self-fulfilling prophecy where our nervous system predicts and then perpetuates hostility. This can easily lead us down a pathway where it feels like children are "choosing to behave badly." In reality, our own fear and worry make us hypervigilant to perceived threat, so we start to see "poor" behavioural choices. The child is likely to experience a similar emotional response and believe they are being picked on and suddenly the situation rapidly escalates.

There have been many times in my career when I have co-regulated a child, brought their pre-frontal cortex back on-line, discussed with them what happened and what went wrong before finally managing to bring them back to the member of staff so that repair can take place. However, all too often, the member of staff hasn't been co-regulated or managed to self-regulate. This often leads to them again reprimanding the child, sometimes in front of another member of staff, in search of validation. The child then "flips their lid," and we are back to square one. This highlights the need for schools to carefully support staff and students with a shared understanding of the restorative process. It highlights the need to make sure everyone has the opportunity to either co- or self-regulate and ultimately leads to a happier and safer working and learning environment.

The opportunity for repair through a restorative approach encourages forgiveness, understanding, and personal growth. Children thrive in environments where they feel a sense of belonging. A relational approach prevents lasting shame and further trauma, nurturing a more compassionate and inclusive community where all members can flourish.

A willingness to invest time and energy into building relationships and displaying empathy are crucial for the development of neural networks in the child's brain, which in turn sustains long-term improvement in behaviour. This can only be achieved if this process becomes embedded within school culture. At every level, from leadership to support staff, consistency is key.

In Chapter 2, I described a situation where a child stormed out of a classroom and then kicked the form tutor's door to get their attention. Whilst the form tutor had been very respectful and had an excellent relationship with the child, they failed to remind the child that kicking doors was unacceptable. Consequently, the child learned nothing from the situation. Although there was no actual damage caused, pre-emptive preventative work could have taken place. This was a perfect opportunity to provide a learning opportunity which might help abate escalation in the future. It is likely that in this situation, the teacher was trying to "keep a lid" on the child's behaviour and prevent it from escalating. They also probably wanted to avoid getting involved in an altercation that might damage their relationship with a very complex child. It is possible that the teacher was worried that addressing the behaviour at that moment might result in less control over the child's future actions.

However, for meaningful and sustainable behaviour change, it is essential that staff members consistently "set limits" on behaviour and provide clear guidance, especially when challenging situations occur. This approach not only helps shape positive behaviours but also reinforces the importance of accountability and respect.

We need to work on building and developing teacher confidence so that they are comfortable in addressing behavioural issues with compassion. If staff see such incidents as an opportunity to model for the child which behaviours are acceptable, which are not, and why this is the case, there is much more chance for repair and understanding. We need to help our staff recognise that their positive relationship with the child is a strength that can be trusted and is not something that is fragile and will break if they hold the child to account. The member of staff might have mistakenly believed that they were expected to "tell the child off" for kicking the door. This is not the case. Nor were they being asked to create confrontation to address the child's instinctive response to kicking the door. Having recognised that the child was in an agitated state, the teacher needed support in being confident enough to address their actions in a non-confrontational way. This doesn't have to be a reprimand or a threat.

As discussed earlier, when a child is in an agitated state, they are not receptive to reason. They have "flipped their lid," and for any meaningful conversation or learning to take place then it is necessary to reconnect the pre-frontal cortex. The teacher approached the situation correctly, until the very end. They should have greeted the child with warmth and empathy, whilst also modelling clear expectations. For example, "I imagine you are feeling very frustrated and of course I can help you but let's not kick the door now, huh? That's not the best way to get my attention." This way the child learns that no matter how they are feeling, certain behavioural choices are not acceptable.

All my staff are trained in the use of Emotion Coaching based on the work of Gottman et al. (1996). When I attended the training, provided by Emotion Coaching UK, I experienced a light bulb moment as it was the first time I had been taught about neuroscience, how this led to certain behaviours, and, more importantly, what we could do to better meet the needs of children. The work of Gilbert et al. (2021) explains how to use the four-step process of Emotion Coaching:

Step 1: Recognising the child's feelings and empathising with them.
Step 2: Labelling the feelings and validating them.
Step 3: Setting limits on behaviour if needed.
Step 4: Problem-solving with the child.

(Gilbert et al. 2021)

Will this immediately prevent the child from kicking doors in the future? Probably not. But if all staff maintain good relationships with the child, and consistently set limits on their behaviour, in time the child will learn to manage their anger appropriately. It is not necessary for the member of staff to confront the pupil, publicly rebuke them, or "fall out" with them. As trusted adults, our words carry weight and can have a lasting positive impact on the children's behaviour. As Dr Jody Carrington said "A traumatised child doesn't need an adult who is trauma informed yet still behaviour focused."

Showing compassion never means accepting bad behaviour, in fact, it means exactly the opposite. It involves counselling the child respectfully and at the right time, teaching them how to manage their emotions and understand which behaviours are unacceptable. Showing compassion often means giving difficult messages empathetically.

Often due to many external pressures, schools focus on curriculum delivery and content and forget that it is also necessary to teach children how to manage their behaviour. Punitive approaches do not *teach*.

"If a child doesn't know how to read, we teach."
"If a child doesn't know how to swim, we teach."
"If a child doesn't know how to multiply, we teach."
"If a child doesn't know how to behave, we ... Punish."
(John Herner, National Association of State Directors of Special Education President 1998-1999)

Part 3 – Rules

To create a culture of compassion in our schools, we need to understand and appreciate how complicated a set of rules may appear to children. I have often heard secondary school colleagues argue that "students should know how to behave by secondary age." However, there is often disagreement over rules among staff and inconsistency in their application. As I have stated previously, consistency is key and if staff can't agree on which rules to follow whilst turning a blind eye to others, then what chance do the children have of truly understanding what is expected of them? Staff may "bend the rules" for a whole manner of different reasons. For example, a school may enforce the rule that children must not wear coats in the building. If, for example, it is particularly cold, some staff may sympathise and allow the children to wear their coats in that lesson, whereas another member of staff may enforce the rule whatever the conditions. In this situation, neither member of staff is wrong, but the message is unclear for children which can lead to conflict.

I worked in a school where some teachers let children charge their phones whilst other vociferously would not. Equally, there was a situation where a child was waiting for an important phone call (with regards to a very serious operation outcome) but their battery was low and so they had asked the teacher if they could charge their phone. Staff must make on the spot decisions and by the nature of this, these decisions are not always consistent with other staff or in line with a behaviour policy. Sometimes staff are making decisions based on need; sometimes on empathy; sometimes in a trauma responsive way; sometimes they are enforcing school rules. Some of these decisions are well informed;

some of these decisions are ill-informed; sometimes they are to keep the peace and sometimes they are to avoid conflict.

There are times when, unfortunately, it is the teachers who further exasperate the children's difficulties, likely due to the pressures they face. Some teachers publicly "call out" or try to shame children. This is sometimes when the adult's nervous system is threatened and so the adult reverts to their child state. I've witnessed many situations where a teacher puts a child in a position of having to "choose" between obeying the teacher or entertaining their friends. Inevitably, in most of these cases, entertaining friends wins.

To further complicate this, children face a multitude of different rules that can be contradictory. They often have a set of rules at home, a set of rules with their friends, and a set of rules in their community. This is made more confusing by the fact that the rules they had at primary school are likely to be different to the rules they have at secondary school. If a child has had multiple school moves, this issue is further heightened.

We must also consider the fact that "many pupils have not yet arrived at a stage of development where that have internalised the moral rules that the school is attempting to inculcate" (Durkheim, 2011). We are expecting children to internalise and accept multiple sets of rules which actually require a fully matured brain to process. Since key developmental changes which "rewire the brain" take place during adolescence and the brain's transition from childhood to adulthood isn't complete until roughly 25 years of age, it's not surprising that adults, adolescents, and children find themselves in conflict with each other.

In nearly every school I have worked in, on the first day of term, the children are called to an assembly where they are told by senior staff that the school "expects compliance." At the same time, they are subconsciously grappling with the intricacies of all the different rules which surround them. It's not surprising that schools experience "behavioural" difficulties. There isn't a single set of rules that can create the perfect school and ensure that all children behave at all times.

How do we make sense of this? What are we supposed to do? Without guidelines we run the risk of slipping into chaos but a purely rule-based system doesn't work. If we are not careful, rules quickly back us into a corner. If a rule is broken, it implies that some form of remedy is necessary. A behaviourist approach implies that breaking a rule is a conscious choice and so deserves punishment. But "If we try to diminish a behaviour by mild punishment and it does not prove effective, the logical step is to try more severe punishments" (Skinner, 2002) and then "a focus on punishment may serve to generate compliance rather than self-regulated behaviour" (Kohn, 2018).

We must also accept that there are a whole host of reasons why some students will struggle to conform to the expected norms of behaviour. This might be because they are hypervigilant due to trauma; it might be because of attachment issues; it could be because they are neurodivergent. It is also important to acknowledge that it is often these same students who may struggle to integrate or make friends within their school community.

With a rule-based system, some schools feel they must apply a tariff-based consequence regardless of all the above, reducing a child's sense of belonging and further isolating them when they need support the most.

As a senior leader, it is not uncommon for a generally red-faced and dysregulated child to appear at your office, accompanied by an equally red-faced and dysregulated member of staff. The member of staff is often so cross and indignant that they must recount their version of events of rule breaking in front of the child. They have often sidestepped the pastoral team and the behaviour system to bring the child straight to your office. When they are in such a heightened state of dysregulation, they generally want some kind of immediate consequence and vindication. This is not a criticism; I have done the same thing multiple times. Equally as a senior leader I have experienced such visits more times than I can count.

On one occasion, later in the day, following a similar incident as described above, the member of staff asked, "What happened to the child?" This is also a very common question. Until we have systems in place in schools to co-regulate both staff and children this will continue to happen. My school wasn't yet in a place where Relational Inclusion was fully embedded and understood. I explained that the child had been with me for over an hour, and we had discussed what had happened, why they felt this had happened, and how they were going to repair the harm. The member of staff was not happy at all and responded, "You've just given the child the attention that they were after!"

It is so important to reflect on that sentence. I can absolutely understand the frustration the member of staff was experiencing and expressing; however we must again think carefully about what it is that we want and whose needs are being served by the outcome. Dysregulation prevents rational thought. As professionals working with children, surely the best outcome lies with supporting the child in understanding what has happened, why it happened, and how it can be repaired. The intention is that, down the line, this will change the pattern of behaviour for the better. Again, this does not happen overnight; it takes time, conscious effort, and patience.

In the example outlined above the child did everything that they said they would do to repair the harm. Although it wasn't the last bit of misbehaviour that we had to endure, they were well respected by staff by the time they left school, and they even came back a year later to thank everyone for their help in getting them into college. Isn't that the best outcome for everyone?

Unfortunately, schools also use a variety of forms of exclusion as their consequence system because this is the system we know; this is what is familiar. Decisions are often made from a punitive mind-set and sometimes are the result of pressure. If headteachers are perceived to not be supporting and backing their staff, if children are not being "punished" for their misdemeanours, there can be a misguided fear that "the highest standards are not being met and chaos will ensue." As well as balancing staff expectations, school leaders also must appease those of parents. And most of us came through an education system which didn't understand the workings of the brain.

Exclusion can take many forms. Children may be excluded from lessons in the form of internal isolation. They may be suspended from school for a specified period of time. There is often a feeling that certain behaviours clearly demonstrate that some children can't behave and so should be excluded from sporting activities or enrichment activities such as school trips and visits. Activities such as these are often viewed as privileges. School leaders and staff may feel compelled to withhold these opportunities, concerned that "rewarding" perceived misbehaviour could send the wrong message to other students and undermine the very fabric of the discipline model expected within a school environment.

If we consider the pupil profile tool described in Chapter 5 and the need for compassion described earlier in this chapter, we can start to see why such rigid approaches offer no support, no chance for learning, no opportunity for repair, and consequently little chance of the child being able to make any significant change to their behaviour. Children who are hypervigilant are "surviving not living" (Phillips et al., 2020) and it is these children who may benefit the most from sport and enrichment. Why, as a society, do we feel the need to punish them twice? As the

African proverb states: "the child who is not embraced by the village will burn it down to feel its warmth."

A Possible Way Forward

From a whole school perspective, we should think in terms of "expectations" as opposed to hard and fast rules. We should try to keep the number of expectations to a minimum and keep them short and precise. We need to discuss, define, and revisit the expectations regularly so that their meaning is clear and understood by all stakeholders.

Paul Dix (2016) recommends three clear expectations: Ready, respectful, and safe. In one of my schools we developed this into The Three Bees:

- Be ready
- Be respectful
- Be safe

We qualified this with a clear explanation:

> The Three Bees mean treating others and the environment with respect, recognising when we are ready to learn and what strategies we need to put in place if we are not, and ensuring that everyone is kept safe.

These expectations should be echoed in individual classrooms. Teachers can explore each expectation with their classes, discussing and modelling what they look, feel, and sound like.

It is also important to avoid using the expectations as a shaming tactic. When a child is dysregulated, for some reason our instinct is often to fire questions at them: *Which expectation are you breaking? What does this expectation mean? Do you understand our expectations? How could you do this better?* If we bombard a dysregulated child (or adult) with questions, their amygdala will simply follow its fight or flight pattern. All these questions can be explored. But only once the pre-frontal cortex is back in control.

As adults, we must create time to regulate our own nervous systems and think through what we really want the focus and outcome of the conversation to be. We can then shape our discussion around expectations and what the barriers to meeting them are as opposed to blaming the child for choosing to break rules. It is not always easy to recognise when we have become dysregulated. In my school we introduced "the blue folder" as a co-regulation strategy. If a member of staff recognised that another member of staff was becoming dysregulated, they would ask them to go and collect a "blue folder." This was a signal for them to take themselves out of the situation allowing a more regulated member of staff to step in.

By focusing on expectations rather than rigid rules, we create an environment where children can learn from their mistakes without feeling ostracised or unfairly punished. This approach fosters a compassionate culture geared towards understanding and supporting the emotional and cognitive development of children and young people. This perspective recognises that children are in the process of growth and brain development; they are doing their best to interpret the world and their place in it.

When children do make mistakes and so are unable to meet the agreed expectations, it is important to name the action, not the child, when we address this. We shouldn't say, "Adam you are violent." Or "Adam you are selfish." Or "Adam you are mean." Language like this induces shame and puts the emphasis on the child as a person as opposed to the action they are responsible for. This approach makes children feel that it is them who are "bad" which can retraumatise the child and can be very difficult to repair. If, instead, we name the action which isn't meeting the expectation, we allow the child to see that they are able to work with an adult on repair. This process enables learning and growth.

For example, we may say, "Adam, I imagine that you are feeling very cross, but tipping over tables is not a good way to make you feel better. It makes the classroom unsafe and some of the other children might feel scared."

Here we focus on the act of tipping over tables as this is where Adam is not meeting expectations. It is not "him" as a child who is violent, it is his action which is making the classroom unsafe. When phrased in this way Adam is able to see that the actions he has chosen are the cause of the problem whilst allowing him to still feel he is a valuable member of the community.

Part 4 – Parents and Community

Children learn a great deal from their parents, who themselves have learned from their own parents. Parents may be dealing with their own trauma, either directly or as a result of intergenerational trauma. If schools, parents, and communities can work together cohesively to provide a consistency of approach and understanding, this can only improve the way our children and young people enjoy and experience the world. "Good enough parenting" has significant impact on a child's life. We must also recognise that many of our families and communities have experienced significant trauma in the past or are experiencing real trauma in the present. Whereas the deficit narrative discussed in Chapter 5 would apportion blame here, it is vital we learn from the mistakes we have made historically. Family trauma can negatively influence childhood development; however if we work together, we can be proactive in our support. Understanding the underlying socio-dynamics is crucial in nurturing a child's growth and interpreting their behaviour within the context of their diverse experiences.

Children observe how family members interact with each other and the wider world, forming their own conclusions about the effectiveness of these behaviours. This is one of the factors in how they create their internal working model. If a parent's learned behaviour is to resort to screaming and shouting to feel seen and heard, it's no surprise that the child might adopt the same approach. Similarly, if a child is raised with the belief that they should retaliate harder if someone hits them, it's understandable that they may get into trouble for fighting at school. Over time, "emotional states become personality traits" and then it becomes difficult to separate the behaviour from the person.

I had just begun my role as a headteacher when a child was brought to my office for making homophobic remarks towards a male teacher. At a later meeting the parent and their child arrived punctually; they were well-presented and polite. They came into my office, listened respectfully, and nodded at all the right moments as I described the incident, explained why the child's behaviour was unacceptable, and outlined the consequences.

Once I had finished speaking, the father responded by saying, "I hear what you are saying, but I encourage my son to be homophobic. I don't think it is right and *they* should not be allowed to work in schools."

As headteachers, we find ourselves placed in many challenging and unexpected situations. We see and hear things that we just can't predict. His response took me totally by surprise. Unsure of what to say next, I explained why I believed such behaviour was wrong and how it is viewed in the eyes of the law and noted that for his child to function in school, such views needed not to be voiced. The parents and the child agreed, and "life" went on as normal.

The irony is that as punishment for his behaviour, I suspended the child for a day. I had forced the child to stay at home with a family who encouraged and validated this kind of behaviour. This is often the hidden worry and consequence of suspension; as a punishment or consequence we place children into the very environment which is causing them harm.

Removing punitive approaches to behaviour, as I believe all schools must do, does not mean allowing children to misbehave. It does not mean that schools will become like the Wild West. Although teaching children to understand, confront, and deal with their emotions can be very challenging, teaching them to understand when someone is feeling vulnerable or is not coping with their emotions can only have a positive and lasting impact on them and the whole of society. I remember being told by a very experienced teacher that what mattered wasn't the severity of the consequence, but the fact that it wasn't being ignored.

The way that children respond to a relational approach is also interesting. One of my fondest memories is when one of my older students, standing well over six feet (in height and width), came storming into my office. His face was red, and he was furious. I scanned the room for things that might get thrown at me but unfortunately, the chairs were nearer him than they were me. I was pretty sure I was not going to be able to usher him out of the room. Incensed with rage, he could barely get his words out. He started to tell me about an incident that had taken place the previous day where he had been very unkind and physically aggressive towards another pupil. He told me about all the other pupils who were involved and how, when he was asked about it, he realised that what he had done was not appropriate and he "fessed-up." More to the point he was proud to have been the only one who took responsibility for their actions.

"So why," I asked, "did he feel so angry now?"

His response still makes me smile.

He said, "Because now I have got to f***ing reflect on it!"

How I remained professional I really don't know. He left my office and completed a period of reflection, which involved talking though the incident with a staff member and discussing how to repair the harm.

A Stepped Approach

As opposed to a rigid tariff system, there is another way we can support our children and young people. The "stepped approach" doesn't always take place in one day or even in a week. It recognises the state a child is in and works with them at a pace which responds to their needs. Equally the issue is always addressed, and the process of repair is modelled until it becomes embedded. It takes different amounts of time depending on what has happened and what point of regulation the child is experiencing.

In the schools I have worked with, time is often raised as an issue and a barrier. There just isn't enough "time" to do everything. However, when a child is dysregulated, to them, "time" doesn't matter, it's immaterial. Just think about what happens when a child dysregulates. Generally, it takes "time" to tell them off. This stops the whole class learning as the teacher must focus their attention on a particular child. If the child doesn't respond to early reprimand and threat of a punitive consequence, more "time" is taken. The teacher now must decide what to do next. Sometimes they must send for another member of staff or senior leader. This takes up more "time." The senior leader may have to remove the child from the class. This may or may not be effective or adhered to, and now another member of staff's "time" is taken. And then, of course, there is the follow up. This might involve detention or isolation, if may involve parental meetings, it may be escalated to the headteacher or even a governing body panel. All of this takes an increasing amount of precious "time" and sometimes this "time" is wasted as the same behaviour is demonstrated the next day and the next. Relational Inclusion provides us with a different way of using the same *time*. With this approach we might just be able to avoid the feeling of "Groundhog Day."

Step 1 – Protect

The first thing we must always do is make sure that the child is safe. We can't just tell them this; they must feel it. We must ensure that their environment is safe, try to recognise the emotion they are experiencing, empathise with them, and then "soothe to calm."

The first step in de-escalating stress is to remove the child from the situation, to a space that is calm. This is not a punitive measure; it is done in a non-shaming way, protecting their dignity whilst they are in the super-heightened state of anxiety, stress, and anger. Very often, in the moment, the child is completely unaware of their actions.

The child or young person is always taken "somewhere with someone" – to a quiet place with an emotionally available adult or a present, focused caregiver, who can help them co- and then self-regulate and lessen their stress levels.

Step 2 – Relate

To begin the process of co-regulation we must validate the child's feelings. We can do this by naming the emotion that is likely to be underpinning their behaviour. For example, we might say, "Bradley, you look really angry today."

For this process to work we must be non-judgemental, empathic, and curious about what happened. We must accept and validate the emotions beneath the child's behaviour. We might say something like, "I can hear that it is very annoying when that happens. Yes, I can see why that might make you very angry." The aim here is to create a connection with the child or young person before we make any attempt to address the issue. We are looking for connection before correction.

Step 3 – Regulate

Next, we should support the child by encouraging them to use their self-regulation strategies. This might be kicking a football, having a cold drink, eating something crunchy, or time in a calm room. We should remember to praise them for their use of self-regulation skills.

The child must feel safe to move from their highly stressed fight, flight, or freeze response to a state of social engagement when they can be supported to co-regulate. We should co-regulate with them, helping them to relax and be calm. Often, play-based or art-based activities can be used to help decrease the high levels of stress hormones the child or young person is experiencing. This is not rewarding poor behaviour; it is a necessary developmental experience to enable their capacity to reflect.

Step 4 – Reflect

For step 4, we should problem-solve with the child when they are ready to reflect. We should be curious about the possible reasons behind their emotion. We might say, "I wonder if these angry feelings are because you're feeling left out." We should show empathy and acceptance of their feelings, "I get it. I would feel angry if I was feeling left out too."

Often, children and young adults who have experienced ACEs or other trauma suffer from alexithymia (emotional blindness) and so are unable to identify, explain, or describe their emotional state. They have no previous experience vocalising or talking about what is happening to them, or what has happened in the past. They literally don't have the words to explain it. The emotionally available adult helps them to mentalise, interpret, and understand their behaviour psychologically, in terms of exploring their underlying thoughts, feelings, wishes, and intentions.

Once the child is regulated, we can help them begin to reflect and unpick what happened, running through the series of events and discussing their thoughts, feelings, and behaviour.

Step 5 – Repair

Where there has been a rupture in the relationship between a child and a member of staff, the staff member should lead the act of repair of this relationship, so that the child knows that the "relationship is bigger than the act."

It is so important to repair the relationship. We should model for them how to take responsibility for their part in what happened: "I'm so sorry I had to remove you from the classroom. I imagine that was difficult for you, but I could really see you weren't managing."

Where appropriate, together we can help them to reflect on how to put right what went wrong. This should be instigated by the child at an appropriate time and allows for reconnection and recovery, re-joining the class, and reconnecting with their teacher. We should not force a child to apologise as this can be detrimental and cause further shame for them.

We should use repair to set limits on behaviour. We can do this by using correction or problem solving where appropriate. We might say, "I understand that you were cross, but it was not okay to kick the door like that. Let's think about what you could do next time that you are feeling angry." This is supporting the child by providing strategies which will enable them to learn from their experience and ultimately self-regulate in the future.

(This is based on work from Trauma Informed Schools UK and Emotion Coaching UK.)

Reflection

- Are schools struggling with some children's apparent lack of compliance?
- Are schools escalating consequence after consequence with limited impact on changing long-term behaviour?
- Are schools concerned by the amount of time current behaviour systems and practices take?
- Is this impacting on the mental health and well-being of all stakeholders?

Schools will have to work hard to move towards a culture of compassion and repair. If, as a school leader, you decide to change your approach from one that is based on punishment to one that is more compassionate, then you will need to think carefully about how you change the culture, and the way people think in your organisation. It is so important to support staff, through a thoughtful and thorough training package, so that they are fully onboard. If there is any inconsistency it can be confusing for children. There cannot be a limit to compassion, nor can certain behaviours be exempt. As the saying goes, "you can't be a little bit pregnant." It takes time to build the understanding and skills necessary for this approach to be truly effective. Staff and children will always be a product of their own upbringing and belief systems. Please don't be put off, the rewards of Relational Inclusion are immense for all stakeholders. Every training session I have delivered is followed by a member of staff who confidently reports that it has made them re-think their own approach to teaching, relationships, and parenting and the successes they have had.

It is essential for schools to recognise that making mistakes is a natural part of the learning process and does not define a child as a bad person. After all, as Louis Szekely (a comedian) said, "If you went back and fixed all the mistakes you've ever made, you would erase yourself." Instead of focusing solely on punitive measures, schools should emphasise the importance of learning from mistakes and understanding the emotions and thought processes that lead to certain behaviours. By creating a supportive environment where children feel validated and understood, they can begin to develop stronger emotional regulation skills and more effective coping strategies.

It is crucial for the adults in a child's life, including educators, to demonstrate vulnerability and empathy in their interactions. I have often told the young people that I have worked with that you don't stop making mistakes when you become an adult. Mistakes can happen at any time and are a feature of life. The important thing is to learn from our mistakes. By acknowledging our own imperfections, we can create a safe space for children to open up about their own experiences and seek guidance on developing healthier responses to challenging situations.

To make significant and lasting changes in children's lives, not just in school, but in their entire world, we must transform the culture in our schools. We can achieve this by fostering a culture of compassion through Relational Inclusion.

References

Bombèr, L. M. (2020). *Know me to teach me: Differentiated discipline for those recovering from adverse childhood experiences.* Worth Publishing.

Desautels, L. L. (2020). *Connections over compliance: Rewiring our perceptions of discipline.* Wyatt-MacKenzie Publishing.

Dix, P. (2016). Pivotal education. https://www.headstartkernow.org.uk/Paul%20dix%20How-to-Write-an-Outstanding-Behaviour-Policy-2016.pdf

Durkheim, É. (2011). *Moral education.* Dover Publications Inc.

Gilbert, L., Gus, L. & Rose, J. (2021). *Emotion coaching with children and young people in schools: Promoting positive behavior, wellbeing and resilience.* Jessica Kingsley Publishers.

Gottman, J. M., Katz, L. F., & Hooven, C. (1996). Parental meta-emotion philosophy and the emotional life of families: Theoretical models and preliminary data. *Journal of Family Psychology, 10*(3), 243–268. https://doi.org/10.1037/0893-3200.10.3.243

Kahneman, D. (2011). *Thinking, fast and slow.* Farrar, Straus and Giroux.

Kohn, A. (2018). *Punished by rewards: The trouble with gold stars, incentive plans, a's, praise, and other bribes.* Mariner Books.

Mandela, N. (1995, May 8). *Speech at the launch of the Nelson Mandela Children's Fund, South Africa.* Nelson Mandela Foundation.

Phillips, S., Melim, D., & Hughes, D. A. (2020). *Belonging: A relationship-based approach for trauma-informed education.* Rowman & Littlefield.

Roberts, L. (2024). *Leading schools and sustaining innovation.* Routledge.

Siegel, D. J. & Bryson, T. P. (2011). *The whole-brain child: 12 revolutionary strategies to nurture your child's developing mind.* Delacorte Press.

Skinner, B. F. (2002). *Beyond freedom and dignity.* Hackett Publishing Co, Inc.

de Thierry, B. (2019). *The simple guide to attachment difficulties in children.* Jessica Kingsley Publishers.

Trauma Informed Schools UK. (n.d.). *Practitioner training trauma and mental health informed schools and communities – delegate programme handbook.*

Chapter 8

System Change and the Golden Thread

Over the course of my career, I have witnessed a whole host of initiatives emerge and fade away within the educational landscape. Whilst recognising the good intentions behind most of these changes, to enhance outcomes for our young people, it remains evident that successive governments have struggled to adequately address the educational needs of many young people who have not had the best start in life.

Despite funding and initiatives such as the Pupil Premium, designed to allocate more resources to those from disadvantaged backgrounds, the focus within schools still needs to shift from mere financial assistance to developmental support. There needs to be a real spotlight on understanding and supporting the mental health needs of young people, as this is what will enable many to better succeed in life. The current attempts to provide mental health training in schools are admirable; however, we can already see that they become little more than sticking plasters when behaviour policies still require children to be "punished" for being dysregulated.

Some educational leaders still fall short in their understanding of the unique needs of dysregulated children. Subsequently they have failed to implement a range of consistent policies to support all learners, providing mixed messages. With one hand they offer "care and support" for the child, whilst with the other they dish out harsh punishments when the child is struggling.

Some years ago, I proposed trauma training to an organisation, only to be informed that "they had already done that training" some years earlier. On a different occasion, I worked in a school which invested significant funds and staff time in "Restorative Justice" training yet not one policy, procedure, or practice changed in terms of their approach to the young people. As a leader in that school at the time, I bear full responsibility for this oversight.

DOI: 10.4324/9781003532866-9

Too many schools, quite understandably, find themselves rooted in an initiative-driven culture. This is problematic on a number of levels, not least because it leads to the idea that once training has taken place and a bit of tracking or monitoring has happened, the initiative is "done," and so schools move onto the next thing without any real change actually having taken place. Relational Inclusion cannot be just another initiative. It cannot be "done." It must become a core principle of all aspects of our work. It cannot stop when there are exams or when Ofsted visit or when there is a global pandemic. Many years ago, I was asked by my headteacher if I could "do" literacy. I asked him if he wanted this "doing by Christmas" or whether he was committed to long-term change, which would require sustained commitment and would need to remain a priority for the foreseeable future. I can't quite remember but I imagine he rolled his eyes. Sadly, schools live in a space where there are so many priorities that each year something must give to make room for the next thing. This is simply not sustainable.

As Malcolm X (1964) said: "Education is the passport to the future, for tomorrow belongs to those who prepare for it today." The importance of schools creating an inclusive environment for all pupils and the need for the government to provide the structure and regulatory framework that prioritises inclusivity to shape a better and more equitable future for tomorrow cannot be underestimated.

***

Inclusion Isn't Just the Absence of Exclusion

By this point in the book, I would hope that you understand why relationships are key, why a relational approach is necessary, and how an understanding of neuroscience can help us to interpret the needs of our children and support us in developing strategies for better meeting their needs. This chapter will explore why *Relational Inclusion* must be the golden thread that runs through every aspect of our schools. For this to happen there must be a sustained commitment to revamping policies and practices. We must establish a robust foundation for continuous improvement that isn't afraid to tackle issues which have previously been swept under the carpet.

Recently, my school held some training to review our approach to conflict resolution. We have been working on this for some years, but concrete development seems to have been thwarted at every stage. This has been partly due to staff churn and then, of course, there was a global pandemic. I have been wanting us to develop a model of education which recognises the emotional health and well-being of students, the importance of peaceful schools, and how to allow students and staff to recognise and manage their emotions in conflict situations to achieve peace in their school communities.

Dr Luke Roberts led the training, and we discussed the notion that "Peace is not just the absence of war." When there were incidents of conflict in my schools, I wanted to find a way of ensuring a resolution was reached so that true change occurred as a result of a genuine understanding of the underlying issues. I wanted to create a change which enabled education to be a force for social justice in society; that what we modelled in schools would transfer into how our children and young people behaved in their wider society. As educators we have all been in the position of trying to resolve conflict between two children after they have fallen out. But how many times do we hear ourselves say, "If you can't be friends, then just stay out of each other's way!" This is the key to unlocking one of the problems we face. Currently we do not invest the time and effort needed to address the issues which underpin the conflict; instead we seek the instant gratification of "sorting out the problem." The reality is that although the immediate problem has been solved, the child is no better able to understand the feelings of others or solve areas of conflict when it arises in the future. Staying out of each other's way is not a long-term solution. But how do we remedy this?

When I first delved into the realms of trauma and attachment, I was searching for practical strategies that could be applied universally by all staff to better meet the needs of every child. My journey led me to Emotion Coaching training (delivered by Emotion Coaching UK), an experience that had a profound impact on me. Through this training, I gained insight into the underlying reasons for children's reactions and learned how teachers and schools could adapt their responses to support these children in leading more fulfilling lives. Moreover, I discovered that Dr John Gottman, an American psychologist, along with Katz and Hooven (1996), had established a correlation between children whose parents employed Emotion Coaching and improved health, stronger social connections, enhanced academic performance, better behaviour, and increased resilience. The potential benefits were undeniable.

Eager to implement this newfound knowledge, I proceeded to educate all staff on the four key steps of Emotion Coaching, as detailed in

Chapter 7, and provide them with a comprehensive understanding of the methodology's effectiveness. I really believed that this approach would revolutionise the behaviour and success of all our students. However, I soon realised that achieving these goals required more than just training. Despite my conviction and readiness to implement this transformative approach, due to an insufficient understanding, I encountered resistance from some headteachers within my schools. It became apparent that meaningful change could only be realised with the full support and understanding of the entire leadership team. Without leaders setting a precedent for inclusive relationships, the project would inevitably fail.

When we delivered *Relational Inclusion* pilots with a local Trust, I established the direct involvement of the CEO and headteacher as non-negotiable from the outset. Relational Inclusion should not be treated as just another project but rather integrated into the core of school culture and vision. It must remain a constant priority, unaffected by exams or unforeseen crises. The key to achieving this is by maintaining a high level of commitment from school leaders.

Whilst it is important to develop capable teams under the headteacher's guidance, the headteacher themselves must be fully engaged, believe in the principles of Relational Inclusion, and be willing and capable of driving it forward effectively.

Repeatedly, I have been called upon to collaborate with Special Educational Needs Coordinators or pastoral teams to address "problematic" students. To instigate genuine transformation, school leaders must exhibit a sincere dedication to inclusivity, making it a cornerstone of their actions and decision-making processes. This approach should be applied consistently and proactively to benefit all children, rather than simply reacting to issues as they arise.

In order to promote inclusivity, it is crucial to integrate inclusive principles into all aspects of policies and practices within a school. As Dr Luke Roberts would say, "How can we justify isolating children for 'bad behaviour' when our goal is true inclusivity?" This is why it is so important for leaders to ensure that school policies, procedures, and practices consistently reflect and uphold the values of Relational Inclusion. It is vital to regularly assess and adjust policies to identify and then eliminate potential barriers in order to advance equity and inclusivity.

My drive to instigate change stemmed from a desire to better address the diverse needs of children. As theory became practice, I observed both a significant decrease in suspensions and a reduction in the severity of incidents. This led to a dilemma. I had to decide between implementing a no-suspension policy or adopting a more empathetic approach. Recognising the pivotal role of leadership teams in each school and the importance of their support, I understood that not all staff members would embrace such a prescriptive new policy, particularly if they experienced distress or hostility from challenging students.

Instead of implementing a new policy, I encouraged headteachers and staff to explore alternative approaches to addressing behavioural issues, rather than defaulting to suspensions. Through this collaborative approach, suspensions gradually diminished to practically zero. The key here was empowering these teams to skilfully devise alternative interventions when confronted with complex behavioural challenges from students in crisis. When a challenging event took place, our first question became "how will what we do benefit the child?" The impact of this mantra was profound.

During my brief tenure at a Catholic school, I was struck by the daily practice of staff coming together for prayer. The person leading the prayers would consistently refocus everyone on the purpose of their work and the goals they aimed to achieve for the children. This experience left a lasting impression on me, prompting me to question why all schools do not prioritise such "child focused reflections" on a regular basis.

Throughout the years, I have often found myself articulating the same message in various ways to prevent individuals from reverting to old patterns. It is essential to recognise that mere training, communication of behavioural expectations, and policy changes may not be enough to prevent systems from becoming dysfunctional. Continuously realigning staff with the importance of Relational Inclusion will help to solidify and sustain the desired change.

To truly embody inclusivity, we must cultivate learning communities which continuously engage with and respond to new research findings. This will ensure that staff remain informed about the most effective ways to support children's development. It is essential that all new staff members receive a thorough induction on how the school operates and its unwavering commitment to promoting inclusion.

Furthermore, students should actively engage in discussions and activities centred around Relational Inclusion, empowering them to contribute to fostering a welcoming and inclusive school environment. This truly collaborative approach not only enhances the educational experience but also reinforces the values of inclusivity and community within the school setting.

By incorporating these strategies and approaches into the school's practices and core values, we can foster a culture in which Relational Inclusion is not merely an objective but becomes a foundational element of the community's identity and everyday interactions.

This approach may pose a considerable challenge for some school leaders and is unlikely to be accomplished overnight, but the direction of travel must be set. Similarly, we must address the issue of "chosen behaviour," a phrase which has somehow crept into accepted language within schools. I often hear school leaders and staff stating that a particular child is "simply choosing to behave in this manner" – as though the child is consciously trying to cause trouble just for the sake of it. How can they be so certain that this is the case? Which special powers do they possess that I don't? Or is this something else? In the same way that some children don't have the emotional vocabulary to express their feelings, are school leaders and staff really telling me that they feel they have run out of options? Are they finding it difficult to explain to staff who may have been affected that they need to understand the needs of the child and that instant punishment isn't the right solution? After all, we exist within a school system and approach which hasn't changed very much in the last hundred years. This is what we know and what is familiar. It is hard to look at this through a different lens.

For some headteachers, especially when faced with a challenging new school, it is almost common, even expected practice, to establish authority and leadership by signalling a zero-tolerance stance towards disruptive behaviour. The arrival of a new headteacher in my authority usually corresponds with a rise of permanent exclusions for that school in the first year. I remember an internally newly appointed headteacher, upon hearing of their promotion, promptly suspending two children on the same day for displaying challenging behaviour towards them, ultimately leading to their permanent exclusion. This act was evidently intended to establish their position of authority from the outset.

Merely changing policies and procedures isn't sufficient. It is essential that every member of staff in the school embraces these changes or, at the very least, is willing to consistently implement the policies. If there is inconsistency of approach and some staff continue to use outdated methods without being challenged, more than likely the system will break down. Eventually, situations will arise where individuals are faced with either undermining a colleague or trying to appease them, both of which are unsustainable.

Obviously not every member of staff will adhere to every policy perfectly all the time; struggling with a situation or an emotional response is natural and understandable. After all, we are only human. Once, a dysregulated child was kicking a door near my office. Initially, I observed the situation from a distance, noting another staff member was handling it. However, after some time I couldn't concentrate on the work I was doing because of the incessant banging. My patience wore thin. Instead of taking a break, I approached the child and shouted at them to stop kicking the door. To my surprise, the child, unfamiliar with my clear rage, remarked, "Oooh, I can see someone is upset!" This light-hearted response made me chuckle, and order was soon restored. As the trainers at Emotion Coaching UK said: "Not every moment is an Emotion Coaching moment." What is important is that after there has been an event, reflection and repair take place consistently.

Schools which embrace Relational Inclusion as an approach will embark on their own unique journey. This will begin to transform the educational landscape and shape a new future. Below is a non-exhaustive list of areas that schools may consider revisiting to ensure that Relational Inclusion remains the golden thread.

Vision and Values

Schools and trusts must undertake a comprehensive review of their vision and values. When visiting our schools, I was consistently surprised by the number of staff who struggled to articulate our vision and values, despite our best efforts. This led me to wonder how prevalent this challenge might be in other educational settings.

In the early stages of my career, I took part in a marketing course as a staff governor. One of the exercises was crafting a one-sentence vision for the school and listing three core values. Although everyone tried to be original in their thinking, the responses were very similar. They focused on achieving the best results for pupils, maintaining high standards, and helping children succeed in life. The trainer pointed out the lack of difference and practical significance in our responses. From then on, I always question new initiatives with, "Does this truly reflect us?"

Whilst researching this chapter, I googled school vision and values, selecting sources at random. The search outcomes revealed recurring themes such as safety, independence, care, curiosity, respect, and kindness – characteristics that are universally embraced by schools. It is so important for educational institutions to revisit their vision and values. We must assess how our principles manifest in daily practices and ensure they cater for *all* students, especially those who struggle to self-regulate. The critical distinction lies in whether schools adhere to conventional rhetoric or genuinely reflect on how they create an environment suitable for *all* children.

(Staff) Code of Conduct

Earlier, I mentioned the importance of all staff fully embracing a new way of working. One effective method to ensure that all staff align with the school's vision and values is by implementing a strong "staff code of conduct." If any member of staff undermines the school's efforts to better meet the needs of all children, they may require additional support or training. We all have days when we handle situations poorly; throughout this book I have been honest about the mistakes I have made. However, we must create a culture where we reflect on these instances and do our best to repair any harm caused. Thinking it is acceptable to bark orders at children should be firmly relegated to the past.

Training Plans

Schools should revise their "training plans" to ensure that their staff receive regular updates and refresher courses on the guiding principles of Relational Inclusion. It is necessary to find the right balance between repeating training, refreshing training, and providing an opportunity for staff to practice, rehearse, and revisit whilst also keeping up to date with recent research. We must retrain our own nervous system responses as it is natural to struggle to make the right choices when we are under pressure and are experiencing heightened stress. If we create opportunities for groups of staff to analyse case studies and engage in discussions about "real life" challenging situations that they have encountered, this will help them to further develop their toolbox of strategies. I strongly believe that empowering staff through respect and encouraging honest self-assessment brings out their best performance.

Having the experience of working in multiple schools and collaborating with many more, including supporting new school leaders, I have noticed a common trend in their training programmes: The focus is often limited to teachers and teaching assistants, whilst other staff members in the school community are frequently overlooked. I firmly advocate for comprehensive training in *Relational Inclusion* for *all* school staff, including administrative personnel, cleaners, cooks, caretakers, and others. Demonstrating a unified approach and consistent care for students sets a positive example and fosters a culture of shared expectations and standards.

Staff Induction

Every school should conduct a thorough assessment of their "staff induction processes" for new staff members. As outlined in Chapter 2, employing a cultural fit approach during the recruitment process is vital, but support for new staff must extend beyond that initial stage. Beginning a new role can present significant challenges, particularly when there is a wealth of information to grasp within a short timeframe. Although new employees often refer to the staff handbook to gain insights into their duties, the written directives may not always accurately reflect the day-to-day realities of the school environment. Additionally, certain implicit practices that veteran staff members consider common knowledge may not be explicitly documented in formal policies. There should be a consciously crafted staff induction process which takes place consistently throughout the duration of at least the first term after joining a new school.

School Rules

Schools must regularly reassess their "school rules." Rules are discussed in much more detail in Chapter 7. As already said, I recommend replacing the term "rules" with "expectations," as this can shift the focus towards fostering a supportive environment. Schools should also evaluate how these expectations are enforced and communicated to students. Children should learn that mistakes are opportunities for growth and that falling short of expectations is part of the learning process. They should understand that navigating difficult situations is a shared journey where they will receive guidance and support. Additionally, it is crucial for students to feel valued and cared for, fostering a sense of belonging and love within the school community.

Relational Policy

Changing from a **behaviour policy** to a relational policy would represent a significant leap forward for most schools. There is a distinct difference in focus between the two approaches. The former typically emphasises rewards and sanctions, outlining the progressive consequences for violations of school rules. In contrast, the latter prioritises fostering strong relationships and delivering bespoke support tailored to individual need. It sets clear boundaries which "are firm on the behaviour but gentle on the child" (Trauma Informed Schools UK, n.d.). A relational policy recognises that positive behaviour can be achieved through modelling. Equally it views negative conduct as a flag identifying that a child needs support, which will be offered without compromising expected standards.

Writing a behaviour policy leads schools to define what is acceptable and what is unacceptable behaviour. This inevitably leads to focusing on what will happen if a child does not behave. Producing a relational policy encourages schools to think about how to support a child who is struggling with regulating their behaviour. This supportive (as opposed to punitive) approach can lead to an altogether different outcome for the child.

In one school, I established "Support for Learning" areas where an emotionally available, well-trained staff member could assist children in regulating their behaviour in a non-judgemental, safe environment. Children could seek support as needed, or staff could guide them to these rooms for assistance. The primary goal was always to enable the child to return to learning promptly and to help them learn how to manage their emotions more effectively.

Withdrawal Units

Schools need to consider the difference between true *support for learning* and the use of "withdrawal units." Schools rarely call such spaces a "withdrawal unit." They are called "Reflection Rooms" or "Inclusion Centres" or "Respect Spaces." Such names imply schools are providing additional support to children to help them succeed. In my experience, these units move the child out of the main school setting, away from their peers, sometimes to a different location quite far from the main school. Whatever the euphemism, their purpose, in reality, is to "remove the problem" in order to maintain normalcy for the main school population. Schools expect children to attend such "units" until they have learned how to behave, typically for about 12 weeks. Then the children are reintegrated into the main school to resume normal activities. I'd be amazed if anyone can demonstrate a "unit" that effectively teaches a child how to behave within 12 weeks, enabling them to adapt and thrive in an environment that previously posed challenges.

Reasonable Adjustments

Schools must not hesitate to implement reasonable adjustments for children in need. Despite potential pressure from various stakeholders such as local authorities, social workers, Ofsted, or other professionals, it is crucial to stand firm. Some children may struggle emotionally with a full day of school, whilst others may find it challenging to meet the demands of a full timetable. It is essential to recognise that whilst some students may only require temporary adaptations, others may benefit from longer term support. This must not be an excuse for keeping children away from school or used as an alternative to suspension. The reasonable adjustments should be monitored carefully and reviewed regularly but should always be child-centred. We should not be imposing curriculums on children which set them up to fail.

When schools can show that the adjustments made are in the best interest of the child and have the support of the parents, which is typically the case, they deserve commendation for addressing the child's needs rather than resorting to exclusion. I have frequently faced enquiries questioning why a child does not have a full 25-hour timetable. The priority must always be focused on keeping children engaged at an appropriate level. By not allowing a flexible curriculum we run the risk of further alienating the children from their education.

If our aim is genuinely to keep children in school, as opposed to excluding them, we must have a more realistic view of how the curriculum works and how it can be made more flexible. We must be able to make sensible adaptations to meet need. Children are not all the same. They are not products on a factory line. If they can't be in school as a result of trauma or anxiety and they can't be at home because this might not be safe or practical, then we need to address these issues creatively for the good of the child.

Forcing them into environments where they can't succeed or don't feel safe is a ridiculous "square peg round hole" scenario. If we recognise the "cause" early enough, we can support children without hiding behind insufficient excuses.

The Role of Government

If we are going to make real change, schools must embrace an inclusive approach to education, although I am realistic about the challenges. To enable such change, it is essential for the government to establish a framework guiding and supporting all schools as to how this can be achieved. The following section explores how this might be done.

A New Vision for Education

In the last 25 years, schools have gained increasing autonomy, leading to a diminishing role of local and national government in setting education priorities. This autonomy has resulted in multi-academy chains or individual headteachers exerting significant control over our children's education, often without sufficient accountability. Whilst I support the involvement of non-educationalists in educational governance, it is crucial to prevent them from exerting undue influence and imposing narrow and poorly informed views on schools. Merely having received an education does not qualify someone to make educational decisions. In a democratic society, politicians, backed by expert advice and guiding principles, should determine what is best for children. If they fail, the electorate can replace them with individuals who hold different views.

A unified national educational vision is crucial, one that secures broad support and sets the framework for how schools should operate. Whilst diversity and innovation should be embraced, there must be boundaries to prevent schools from disproportionately disadvantaging certain students for the perceived benefit of the majority. Just as hospitals may differ in their functions, a shared national perspective highlights the importance of a healthcare system that offers free services to all in need, regardless of financial status. Similarly, establishing a set of national standards can outline the essential expectations we have for our schools.

This national educational vision must be rooted in the fundamental principle that every school has a responsibility to educate all children, regardless of their background or individual needs. We must move away from the outdated practice where some schools selectively admit students based on various criteria. In today's diverse society, it is crucial that all schools embrace inclusivity and provide an education to every child, ensuring equal opportunities for all. This shift towards universal education not only promotes equity but also fosters a more cohesive and harmonious learning environment for all students, regardless of their circumstances.

The Democratic Deficit

As schools have gained more autonomy, the role of local authorities has become ambiguous, and the involvement of regional directors has further complicated the situation.

Local authorities play a crucial role in delivering essential public services and representing the interests of their communities. These services range from social services and housing to planning and transportation. They support their communities through economic development and regeneration to improve the quality of life and stimulate growth. Local authorities are accountable to their communities through elected representatives, public consultations, scrutiny processes, and transparent decision-making.

However, their role in planning provision for education has become increasingly unclear. How can we have a contradictory system where locally elected representatives may have one vision for education whilst Regional Directors approve school takeovers by trusts with a totally different culture and ethos? There is a need for greater transparency and consistency between parties who should be aligned. Surely a local vision for education must be created collaboratively and not dictated and on occasion overruled by a system with no accountability.

The impact of child poverty on schools exacerbates these challenges. Some schools face higher levels of need, yet the inspection and accountability frameworks do not adequately consider this factor, but more of this later. Equally, schools with oppressive regimes may exhibit higher exclusion rates and manipulate student admissions. This selective approach adds pressure on other schools with high needs, as they end up receiving the students rejected by these schools. Local authorities should establish mechanisms to ensure that all schools can meet the needs of diverse students without creating imbalances. If all schools are expected to accommodate all students, accountability measures would be more equitable across the board.

Improving Accountability

Looking ahead, we must improve outcomes for all children, both nationally and locally. There have been proposals to exempt certain children from school accountability measures, but this is not an idea

I support. Such a measure would neglect the academic needs of those children and may inadvertently incentivise increasing the numbers of those being exempted. It is possible to educate children with behavioural difficulties, and not all students facing self-regulation challenges necessarily struggle academically.

Acknowledging the attainment gap between the most and least advantaged in society, and the ongoing efforts to narrow this gap, is essential. Whilst this book does not delve into the reasons behind the attainment gap, it is worth noting the significant link with poverty. Whilst advocating for reducing inequalities in society, the focus here is on how our accountability measures can better reflect the progress of all students and the schools who do all they can to support children whose needs are not adequately met within the current education system. As already stated, prioritising their mental health needs can greatly contribute to their success and foster social mobility.

Analysing the Progress 8 scores for all schools nationally in 2023 reveals a stark contrast: The average Progress 8 score for disadvantaged students was −0.57, whereas for non-disadvantaged students, it stood at +0.17. Schools with a higher percentage of disadvantaged pupils often encounter greater challenges in achieving a positive Progress 8 score compared to institutions with more affluent student populations, therefore, it may not accurately reflect how well schools cater to the diverse needs of all children.

> More advantaged students will tend to be academically successful despite what we do, whereas the performance of less advantaged students is more likely to be because of what we've done.
>
> What this means is that although you may feel very proud of the results of more advantaged students, they are likely to have been successful regardless of your actions and decisions.
>
> (Didau, n.d.)

Using Progress 8 data alone to evaluate individual schools is overly simplistic and lacks meaning unless the unique context of each school is considered. FFT Education Data Lab has presented insightful findings advocating for a more nuanced approach in utilising progress data. In a study, Katie Benyon highlighted that disadvantaged pupils not only tend to underperform compared to their more privileged peers but also that those experiencing prolonged disadvantage fare the poorest (Beynon, 2023).

Throughout the country, numerous schools demonstrate high levels of free school meal eligibility. Despite having a Progress 8 figure that falls below the national average, these schools often excel in their Progress 8 outcomes for disadvantaged pupils, who represent the majority of their student population. For instance, a local school has one of the highest rates of free school meal eligibility and a Progress 8 figure of –0.15 for all students, compared to the national average of –0.03. However, the figure for disadvantaged pupils at this school stands at –0.23, which is notably better than the national figure of –0.57.

An interesting project led by Katie Beynon and Dave Thomson focused on developing a School Quality Index that incorporates the contextualisation of Progress 8 data (Beynon & Thomson, 2024). Their research revealed that pupils with specific characteristics tend to achieve higher Progress 8 scores, whilst those facing greater disadvantage attain lower scores. We know that greater disadvantage is often associated with higher incidences of ACEs and early trauma. Benyon and Thomson emphasise that neither Progress 8 nor its contextualised version serves as a true measure of school effectiveness; their value depends on how they are applied. They advocate for integrating both contextualised Progress 8 and raw attainment data to present a more comprehensive view of student achievement compared to either metric in isolation.

Ofsted and School Improvement

I can't write a book about *Relational Inclusion* without addressing Ofsted's role in overseeing accountability and school improvement. When I first started teaching, Ofsted did not exist and, possibly surprisingly, I do not advocate for a return to those days. Prior to its establishment, there was significant inconsistency across schools, low expectations, and poor standards, particularly for disadvantaged students. Working in schools in disadvantaged areas pre-Ofsted, I recall being reminded of the importance of taking an attendance register "in case it was needed by the police." I was also frequently told of the need to "keep these kids off the streets." I don't remember having any lesson observations in my first ten years of teaching.

Ofsted should provide the scrutiny and support schools need to have real impact with "all" our children. They should have a clear focus on inclusive practice and recognise the schools that go above and beyond without resorting to suspension and exclusion. They should be driving the "inclusion isn't just the absence of exclusion narrative."

Ofsted must consider addressing the issue of "managing intake," which not only relates to practices such as off-rolling, but also excessive assessments for EHCPs, "excluding" children by placing them in "withdrawal units," and ineffective use of Alternative Provisions. Then they must judge how well schools cater for the needs of vulnerable students. Whilst Ofsted already "assesses" these areas, the current system lacks fairness and equality.

In recent years, I've had numerous discussions with inspectors about the "right provisions for children with challenging behaviours." Again, here the starting point seems to be wrong. There seems to be an acceptance that some children "don't belong in school." Instead, there should be recognition that many children require reasonable adjustments to accommodate their needs and abilities and schools should be allowed to make these without an inspector "counting hours" as opposed to "understanding how need is being met." Additionally, not all children can be "fixed" as discussed in Chapter 4. No school should be beyond scrutiny for the provision made for our most needy and vulnerable children – far from it, there should be greater scrutiny – but inspections should be realistic and considerate. This shouldn't be about "ticking boxes" – it should be a process which places children, as individuals, at the front and centre, and recognises that one size certainly doesn't fit all.

I understand that no inspection process is infallible and that challenges are bound to arise. I can recall several strange experiences with inspectors that should never have occurred. For example, one school invested heavily in unsightly industrial-grade air conditioning throughout its premises. On headteacher interview, I was informed that this decision was made at the insistence of an inspector who deemed the school unfit for purpose due to inadequate air circulation. Surely, air conditioning should not be part of Ofsted's remit. Shouldn't it be a team of qualified experts that determine whether a school building meets the necessary standards?

On another occasion, an inspector acknowledged that the school was making commendable efforts and merely needed "time to improve." They went on to assess the school as "requiring improvement." When pressed, they could not specify what improvements were needed beyond "additional time." I have also participated in inspections where I was told that our SEMH school should "not have to deal with this level of need." None of this seems logical, and schools often hesitate to voice complaints or are ignored when they do. To make matters worse, a negative judgement often leads to further scrutiny, and schools are then evaluated on how they have responded to a "snapshot" judgement made over two days. Sometimes this moves them further away from the actual improvements which need to take place to move the school forward and support the children, young people, and their communities. To voice dissatisfaction following an inspection is often perceived as denial.

Ofsted should adopt a more balanced approach by evaluating how effectively the system supports students facing significant challenges. A comprehensive assessment is necessary to ensure that a school meets the needs of all students without placing an undue burden on other local schools. It would be easy for all schools to simply permanently exclude their "difficult children." Inspections should be wary of any school that demonstrates rapidly improving, or greatly improved results, but has high levels of exclusions. Inspectors should consider whether a school is adequately addressing the needs of individual pupils, regardless of their educational setting. I can cite numerous instances where special schools are justifiably given leeway for making reasonable adjustments, whilst mainstream schools face criticism for not treating all pupils identically.

Inspectors should receive regular training on meeting the needs of students with mental health issues. A society should be judged by how it treats its most vulnerable, and our education system has fallen short in this regard. If Ofsted were to focus on how schools embrace and support students with complex needs, rather than expecting uniformity for all students, it would lead to a more effective evaluation process.

Meeting the Needs of All Children

Whilst the government has made attempts to support mental health services in schools, there seems to be a misunderstanding of the actual level of need. Their own mental health and well-being document even stipulated that this programme was for "mild to moderate mental health issues" (Gov.uk, 2021). What did this mean for schools who have the most vulnerable children with serious mental health issues? When we were offered support through the government initiative and I explained the backgrounds of some of the children in my schools who desperately needed significant help, I was met with responses like, "we are not equipped to meet the needs of your students," or "*you* are already doing everything you can and we cannot provide additional support." Notably, when schools were provided with greater access to mental health services, we were informed that our mental health worker could no longer be retained due to insufficient capacity in the system.

In a previous chapter, I explored the impact of the Warnock Report (Chapter 1) and the ongoing lack of clarity on the most effective ways to address the needs of children with complex requirements. Despite the presence of the Education Endowment Foundation, aimed at supporting schools in improving teaching and learning for the most vulnerable through evidence-based research, this platform presumes a starting point way beyond where some of our children and young people arrive in schools, meaning it may not be ideal to determine the best approach for meeting the needs of such children. A Royal Commission focused on examining how the education system promotes genuine inclusion could significantly contribute to the ongoing discussion. This commission could assess the use of permanent exclusions, especially in primary schools, the implementation of zero-tolerance systems, and how these practices impact on other schools in the community, and indeed children themselves. It could also identify strategies that truly benefit all children and explore the allocation and availability of limited resources for child mental health support. In addition, considering co-locating mental health resources with special schools focused on social, emotional, and mental health needs, which could also serve as training centres for local schools and establish partnerships with university research departments, could be beneficial.

A crucial step towards improvement is to address child poverty. The undeniable link between poor educational outcomes, mental health issues, and poverty necessitates immediate action – and the impact of work to eradicate this would be felt across generations. Many schools encounter families dealing with highly complex needs and various levels of deprivation, requiring support beyond the scope of what they can offer. Efforts to facilitate joint training for school and social care staff, aimed at aligning support for these families and avoiding conflicting messages, could be beneficial. Unfortunately, initiatives like these often face challenges in progressing to implementation and realising their potential benefits.

> It is often said that "mental illness doesn't discriminate" and whilst it can affect even the princes of England, this seems a slightly misleading sound bite. I'm noticing that it certainly tends to disproportionately

cling more to low socio-economic status, which seems important to acknowledge when considering prevention strategies.

(Waterhouse, 2024)

Mental Health Support for Schools

Earlier, I mentioned the importance of schools providing training around *Relational Inclusion* to all staff members. I strongly believe that giving national emphasis to this training, similar to the National Literacy Strategy, would make a significant difference. How can anyone working with children and young people not be taught how the brain develops and how this can be affected by trauma and attachment? Whilst Mental Health First Aid training has been available to schools, having just one trained staff member is insufficient for the collective effort needed. In my experience working with a school in New York, where access to a variety of medical practitioners is available, a common issue is that teaching staff tend to defer to these professionals and may not see mental health as part of their responsibilities. By ensuring that all staff members are trained, everyone can actively contribute to supporting mental health in schools. Like safeguarding, this is everyone's responsibility.

The National Literacy Strategy, implemented in the early 2000s, provided comprehensive training for all teachers resulting in significant positive outcomes, such as 98,000 more children achieving the expected national attainment level in English according to the Department for Education (DfE). This demonstrates the impact that universal training programmes can have when delivered and funded properly.

The introduction of a National Training Programme offering appropriate training to all professionals working with children and young people has the potential to transform the educational landscape. Empowering schools with the necessary knowledge and skills to address the diverse needs of every child through such a programme could lead to positive and lasting effects on the education system.

Alternative Provisions and Pupil Referral Units

I have worked with many Alternative Provisions over the years and have met some very well-meaning and talented people who operate in this sector. They often provide schools with a great service by supporting children who face challenges. The issue with Alternative Provision lies not with the children, but with the schools that may not be willing or able to meet the specific needs of these children. In my opinion, Alternative Provisions should focus on enhancing the curriculum rather than completely removing a child from the traditional educational setting. Whilst I understand that schools may not always be equipped to offer courses in areas like mechanics, hairdressing, or construction, some students may benefit from additional support through mentoring programmes or other specialised services. Unfortunately, schools sometimes resort to Alternative Provisions for reasons other than this.

I believe that it is important for children in Alternative Provisions to still feel a sense of belonging to their school, continue their education in various subjects based on their abilities, and have the opportunity to participate in the full spectrum of school experiences. This should include access to career guidance, personal development, social skills, health education, and relationships and sex education.

All Schools and Colleges

We understand many of the challenges children face arise during transitions between different phases of education. The transition from one school to another can bring about numerous issues that could be alleviated if schools were more attuned to the needs of the students. In my experience, there is often a tendency to assign blame to various schools without taking full responsibility for ensuring a seamless transition. Primary schools may feel disheartened when their most vulnerable students are quickly excluded by secondary schools, whilst secondary schools may wish for better preparation from primary schools to equip students for the transition. I believe that focusing on the needs of the child can offer valuable insights and solutions.

Similar challenges persist as students transition from secondary school to college. Many receiving institutions may claim that the students are not adequately prepared for the academic environment or not "school/college ready," a topic discussed in Chapter 6. Like the primary headteachers I have talked to, I share the frustration of seeing students we have diligently supported leaving school in July and being classified as "Not in Education, Employment or Training" by November. It is essential for all stakeholders to take collective responsibility for these young people and recognise that they may require ongoing support throughout their educational journey and potentially into their professional lives. By acknowledging that these students are not "broken" and so can't be "fixed" but rather need continuous assistance, we can progress towards establishing a more equitable and supportive society.

A Manifesto for Educational Reform

To address the above points, I propose a manifesto for transformative change. Although challenging, I firmly believe that these objectives are attainable for all schools. They entail a fundamental yet necessary shift in how children with diverse backgrounds are supported. Contrary to common assumptions, implementing these changes does not necessarily require a substantial investment in already limited resources. Rather, it primarily necessitates a shift in perspective – one that prioritises the inclusion of all children whilst not condoning disruptive behaviour as acceptable.

A Manifesto for Educational Reform

1. National Vision:
Elected representatives must establish a comprehensive vision for education, outlining a framework within which all schools will operate. Whilst schools may retain some autonomy in developing their curriculum, values, policies, and procedures, they should adhere to standardised expectations and prioritise Relational Inclusion.

2. Royal Commission:
There should be a Royal Commission charged with reporting on all aspects of mental health support for schools and how best to meet the needs of children with complex mental health issues.

3. Democratic Control of Education:
Regional Directors should be directly accountable to locally elected bodies, helping them to shape and implement the localised educational vision.

4. The Role of Ofsted and Local Authorities:
Schools must reflect the diversity of their local communities and not redirect children with complex needs to other schools. Ofsted assessments should focus on how well schools cater to children

with special educational needs and mental health challenges to ensure fair and inclusive practices in all educational settings.

5. Ofsted Oversight of Trusts:
Ofsted should assess all Trusts to evaluate their adherence to the National Vision for Education and their impact on the overall educational landscape.

6. Use of Contextualised Performance Measures:
Performance measures, including a contextualised Progress 8 measure, should recognise schools that provide comprehensive and inclusive support for students with diverse needs.

7. Inclusive Practices:
Schools should establish relational policies centred around fostering positive relationships rather than implementing punitive measures. This signifies a shift towards prioritising positive connections and empathy within school settings to effectively address behavioural issues. Schools should prioritise finding alternative solutions for students requiring additional support. The integration of all pupils within mainstream settings should focus on addressing individual needs, particularly for students facing trauma or attachment issues. The reliance on Pupil Referral Units (PRUs) should decrease, with a shift towards the reintegration of students into mainstream education and providing a comparable educational offer. Pupil Referral Units should instead be used as therapeutic and training support with a focus on keeping children in their parent school.

8. Role of Alternative Provision:
Alternative Provision should complement the curriculum and cater to the diverse needs of students, maintaining connectedness to their referring schools. Students in these programmes should access a broad range of educational opportunities, encompassing personal, social, health, and economic (PSHE) education, relationships and sex education (RSE), and careers education, as well as social activities like participating in school teams and attending school events.

9. Mental Health and *Relational Inclusion*:
Mental health support and *Relational Inclusion* are essential in all schools. National training in Relational Inclusion for all school staff is crucial to effectively address the needs of students with mental health concerns, underlining the significance of promoting supportive and inclusive environments for student well-being. There should also be a plan for rolling this out to parents and the community.

10. Transition Assistance:
All educational sectors should collaborate to ensure a seamless transition for students with special needs, including facilitating their integration into the workforce. Emphasising ongoing support and opportunities for these students' post-compulsory education is crucial for their continued growth and success.

Reflection

- Are schools recognising that true inclusion isn't just the absence of exclusion?
- Are our vision and values generic or do they really reflect our schools?
- Are we prepared to hold ourselves and our staff to account for the changes that desperately need to take place?
- Are we ready to do what it takes to make a local vision for education a reality?

Anyone who has read *Hogfather* by Terry Pratchett will be familiar with the passage which imagines Rumpelstiltskin waking up years later and being bemused by the changes that he sees in society, yet he still recognises a school (Pratchett, 1996). The buildings are the same, the rituals are the same, and nothing has really changed. How much longer do we continue to exclude children? To grow our special schools ever larger because we "can't meet need"?

Having witnessed the evolution of societal norms over a long span of time, I have been struck by the stark levels of racism and misogyny portrayed in old films like James Bond. It is unsettling to realise what was once deemed acceptable on television; thankfully this is now met with universal condemnation by decent individuals. As a young gay person growing up in the 1970s and 1980s, I keenly experienced the impact of prevailing homophobia on myself and my peers.

When we contemplate the past, we often wonder: "How could we have allowed such things to occur?" We have an opportunity to chart a different course for the most vulnerable children in our society. My sincerest hope is that in 10 to 15 years' time, we will look back and the next generation will ask, "You did **what** to people struggling with mental health difficulties?" whilst recognising that the changes to that approach started here.

References

Beynon, K. (2023, January 4). *The long(er)-term impact of long-term disadvantage at school*. FFT Education DataLab. https://ffteducationdatalab.org.uk/2023/01/the-longer-term-impact-of-long-term-disadvantage-at-school/

Beynon, K. & Thomson, D. (2024, May 21). *Contextualising progress 8*. FFT Education DataLab. https://ffteducationdatalab.org.uk/2024/05/contextualising-progress-8/

Didau, D. (n.d.). *How should we view the performance of the most disadvantaged students?* Learningspy. https://learningspy.co.uk/leadership/how-should-we-view-the-performace-of-the-most-disadvantaged-students/

Gottman, J. M., Katz, L. F. & Hooven, C., (1996). Parental meta-emotion philosophy and the emotional life of families: Theoretical models and preliminary data. *Journal of Family Psychology, 10*(3), 243–268. https://doi.org/10.1037/0893-3200.10.3.243

Gov.uk. (2021, June 2). *Promoting and supporting mental health and wellbeing in schools and colleges*. Gov.uk. https://www.gov.uk/guidance/mental-health-and-wellbeing-support-in-schools-and-colleges

Malcolm, X. (1964, June 28). *Speech at the Founding Rally of the Organization of Afro-American Unity, New York City*.

Pratchett, T. (1996). *Hogfather*. Bloomsbury Academic.

Trauma Informed Schools UK. (n.d.). *Trauma informed knowledge and understanding*.

Waterhouse, B. (2024). *You don't have to be mad to work here*. Jonathan Cape.

Epilogue

Although we were once all children, for some reason, as adults, we forget completely what life is like from a child's perspective. I suppose there are so many new things to take in as a child that, as an adult, you forget the stories you told yourself to make the best sense of what was going on with the limited information you had. Growing up happens so gradually that we simply forget what experiencing everyday things for the first time feels like.

When I was about nine, I fell off my bike. No surprise there. I was always falling off something. Somehow this time I managed to get my leg wedged between my handlebars and bike wheel. It wasn't a bad fall by any means, but it left me with a massive green and blue ugly bruise which took up most of my right thigh.

A few days later we travelled to Spain for our family summer holiday. As a child, that bruise really bothered me. I was ashamed of it; I thought people would stare at me; I wanted to hide it. So, in what was probably 100 degree heat, I decided I was going to wear cords all holiday (it was the early 1980s after all and some 1970s fashion had hung over). I think, to make my story of "not liking the sun" more plausible, I decided to wear a jumper and to stay in the shade. I have a photograph somewhere of me peering out from beneath a straw umbrella looking miserable.

I don't really remember either of my parents challenging me. They probably told me I should wear shorts, and when I got cross and argumentative they just left me to it. It either wasn't worth the argument or they just thought I was being odd, and I'd get over it.

I can't say that the event itself was life changing. The bruise healed. The next year I wore shorts. Other than the faded photos of that year's holiday and me dressed like it was the middle of winter in bright sunshine, it was never mentioned again.

However, there is an important lesson here. As a nine-year-old I made certain assumptions as a result of a feeling that was very real to me but no one else seemed to notice or particularly think about. I come from a caring and loving family and this incident just wasn't picked up on or was tactically ignored. This isn't a criticism or comment on my parents' parenting.

As a result of something as innocuous as falling off my bike, I made certain choices and started to populate an emotional map of the world according to my nine-year-old brain. I made some harmless but fairly weird choices and decisions. I made up a rubbish story (or series of lies from an adult's perspective) to cover my tracks and I made myself uncomfortable for two weeks (I can't imagine I was particularly happy sweating in my clothes).

From memory, no one asked why I was doing what I was doing in a way that I could answer.

Hopefully this book will change the perspective we have as adults and help us see how children act and behave through a different lens. It will help us be curious and help children (and adults) feel comfortable enough to talk about what is really going on. However old we are, however wise we think we have become, we never stop learning. *Relational Inclusion* is a new way. It's an *education for everyone*.

Acknowledgements

It's a funny thing, reflecting on a book and thinking about who helped us along the way.

There are thank yous to all these people and probably many more!

Dr Luke – this book definitely wouldn't have happened without you and we're both a little nervous about what you'll make of it.

Dave B – our unofficial editor. We could tell the bits that irked you – in places it made us both smile – but your honesty and thoroughness has been massively appreciated. We think you spent almost as much time on each chapter as we did. That attention to detail – as well as helping us soften some bits that, well, probably needed softening – has been invaluable. We're sorry if some of our paragraphs offended you!

Sonja – I'm not sure I'd have ever got started on this journey if it wasn't for you. And you've been there pretty much every step of the way for the last five years. Even if I've messaged at silly hours.

Carrie – thank you for encouraging me to stay true to what I believed. It meant so much.

Deborah – for letting us try lots of this with your school before we really knew what shape it would take and for the endless discussions and support.

Emotion Coaching UK – for me you really started this journey and inspired me at every stage.

Simon – for backing me right at the start when I shared a half-baked idea which possibly sounded a little bit crazy and for supporting the ideas as they developed, for helping me for push them with schools, and for believing in this way of working – and then for reading about it again in this book.

Karen – for letting me use your MAT as a guinea pig and for your support and backing all the way through.

Maggie and Bill and the Laurel Trust – for believing in me and backing our first part funded research pilot.

Stacey – for listening to me bang on about this for so long that you didn't even need to read it.

Loads of people read chapters and sections – Steve, Sophie, Amy, Shirls (of course), Ruth, Katie, Dave, Gareth, Kate, and Victoria.

Alison – for believing this book could work before we'd written anything – maybe you didn't even know that.

And Grace – for the help with what to do next.

Finally thank you – the reader – if you've got this far. Now take the next step and take it forward and help change the world. Standing still didn't get anybody anywhere.

Every effort has been made to identify and contact the copyright holders of all materials used in this book. Please contact the publisher if there are concerns regarding copyright issues.

Index

Page numbers in *italics* indicate figures, while page numbers in **bold** indicate tables.

accountability 147, 174–75
accountability frameworks 26–30, 174
active listening 122
adrenaline **65**, 82
Adverse Childhood Experiences (ACEs) **41**, 93, 104–05, 111, *112*, 113–14, 176; impacts of 40–42
affect labelling 45, 119
Ainsworth, Mary 90
alexithymia 159
All the President's Men 95
Alternative Provisions 180–81, 183
ambivalent attachment 91–92, 109–10
Angelou, Maya 56
animals/nature 72–73
animal studies 11–12
anxiety 114
assaults 132–33
attachment 125–26, 130
attachment theory 90–94, 109–10
attention deficit disorder (ADHD) 85, 106
Atticus Finch 85
attunement 144
Atwood, Margaret 13
authors: as a novice teacher 14–17; employment interviews 26; experiences teaching 4–6; shouting 13–15, 18; stories 65–68

Automatic Negative Thoughts (ANTS) 7–8; *see also* Negative Thinking Patterns
avoidant attachment 92–93, 110

babies 83, 90–91
BBC, "The School Where Teachers Never Shout at Children" 14
behaviour cycles 7–8; and epigenetics 11–12
Behaviourists 2–3, 150–51; zero-tolerance approach of 18
behaviour management 76, 147, 149; lack of teaching 14–15; and Ofsted 27–29
behaviours 45, 171; attention-seeking 91–92, 103–04, 130; compliance-based approaches to 140–41, 150–51, 160; and dysregulation **48**; and emotions 17–18, 45, **54**, 119; expectations for 46; modelling 52, 147, 171; negatively changed 103; and the nervous system 35; perceived as choices 34–35, **53–54**, 80, 94–95, 97, 101, 132–33, 146, 167; reactive approaches to 50–51, 76; of staff 62–63; stepped approaches to 157–59; tariff behavour systems 2, 34, **47**, 80, 151, 157; and Victorian England 34–35;

see also disruptive behaviours; misbehaviour
Beynon, Katie 176
biophilia 73
Biophilia Hypothesis 73
blue folder 71, 154
boundaries 46, **47**, 120, 171; and behaviour management 76
Bowlby, John 90
Breaux, Annette 36

Carrington, Jody 148
causes *vs.* symptoms, addressing **48**, 50–51, **54**, 132
Ceaușescu, Nicolae 78–79
certifications 126
change, Obama on 1
child focused reflections 166
children 56–57, 121; communicating with 122; with complex needs 96; expressing emotions 119; fearing teachers 61; forgotten perspectives of 187–88; language criminalising 125, 130–36; lost children 102; and "naughty" labels 8–9, 127; reading to 6; Romanian orphans 78–80; and safety 37–38, 45, 53, **54**, 143–44; on teachers 57; and trauma 62, 64, 85; as witnesses 135–36
children's achievements 49
Chugani, H. T. 79
cinemas 98
Clarke, Ken 8
classrooms, twenty years ago 3–4
Climbié, Victoria 25
colleges 181–82
compassion 51, **54**, 145, 148, 154
complex post-traumatic stress disorder (CPTSD) 80–81, 83; *see also* post-traumatic stress disorder
compulsory education 20–21, 56–57
conflict resolution training 163–64
Connections over Compliance (Desautels) 3
consequences **47**
consistent emotional dysregulation 35

co-regulation 42–45, **47**, 87–88, 128–29, 132–33, 146, 151, 158; *see also* self-regulation
corporal punishment 81–82
cortisol **65**
Craig, Duncan 37–38
criminal damage 133
cultural fit 38, **39–40**, 160, 170

daily check-ins 42–44, 71–72, 119, 144
Dead Poets' Society 65
defiance 34–35
deficit narratives 101, 155
democratic deficit 174
Desautels, Lori 3, 19
Dickens, Charles 101
Dickerson, Joshua T. 49
disabilities, hidden 98
discipline 45
disorganised attachment 93–94, 110
disruptive behaviours 20, 58–59, 106; perceived as choices 34–35; and safety 59; *see also* behaviours
Dix, Paul 153
dopamine 59, **60**
dysregulation 30, 44, **48**, 51, 68, 127–29, 151–52; and illness 113–14; punishing 162; and repair 146; staff 52; termed "incident" 131

Education, Health and Support Plans (EHCPs) 20, 23, 95, 177
Education Act (1880) 20–21
Education Act (1981) 22
educational reform manifesto 182–84
educational standards, and school inspections 27
educational thinking 2; *see also* Behaviourists; *Relationalists*
educational vision 173–74, 182
education budgets 95
Education Endowment Foundation 179
emotional blindness 159
emotional control **60**
emotional intelligence 42, 164

Emotion Coaching 148, 164–65, 168
emotions 45–46, 83, 143–44, 156; and behaviours 17–18, 45, **54**; learning to recognize 119, 144, 159; stiff-upper lip 45
empathy 80, 143
endorphins 59, **60**
epigenetics 10–12
Equality Act (2010) 81
"Every Child Matters" policy 25–26
exclusion 152, 178, 184; *see also* permanent exclusions
executive dysfunction 64
executive functioning 59, **60**, 61

facial expressions 89–90
faulty narratives 124
fear 36, 50, 61; and compliance 140; physical aspects of 63
feral, term 133
FFT Education Data Lab 175
fight or flight mode 35–36, 62, 64, 87, 144, 158; teachers 69
fights 87
Five Key Vocabularies 127–30
flexible thinking **60**
"*flipping the lid*" 142, 144, 147–48
float back 86
Flux, Arthur T. 21
following the money 95
forest schools 73–74
freeze mode 88, **89**, 158

Gilbert, Louise 148
Glassman, Charles 33
Gottman, John 148, 164
government roles 173

"Hand Model of the Brain" 141–42
Hanson, Rick 131
"happy" Hormones 59, **60**, 64–65, 69, 74
Harford, Sean 28
headship 76–77
helicopter analogy 58
Herman, Judith 80

"high fiving yourself in the mirror" 56
hindsight 78
historical eras, Yeats on 1
Hogfather (Pratchett) 184
homophobia 155–56, 185
human brains 8, **60**, *79*, 80, 84, 97, 105, 115, 150; and emotions 45; and fights 87–88; "*flipping the lid*" 142; hand model 141–42; and hypo-vigilance **89**; and learning 24; negativity bias 131; neural networks 97; *see also* nervous system
humiliation/shame, as child management tactic 21–22
hyperarousal 106–07, 114, *115*, 116
hypervigilance 35–36, 64, 88–90, 152
hypo-arousal 107–08
hypo-vigilance 88, **89**

"Improving Social and Emotional Learning in Primary Schools" (van Poortvliet) 117–18
impulse control/self-control **60**, 120
incidents 131–32
inclusivity 126, 139, 163, 166, 173–74, 179, 183
Inside Out 89
intergenerational trauma 10, 12
intermittent reinforcement 91–92
"Internal Alternative Provisions" 6
"internal inclusion/exclusion units" 94–95
internal maps 124
isolation 136–37
I Wonder ... I Imagine ... I Notice ... with Empathy *see* WINE

Kahneman. Daniel 8
kindness 33
Knost, L. R. 99

lateness 114
learning: and fear 63–64; and the human brain 24; and safety 58
Levine, Peter A. 85

Lipton, Bruce 125
lost children 102

mainstream schools 96, 178; and special needs children 23, 126
Malcolm X 163
Mandela, Nelson 139
Mate, Gabor 10
memory 135
mice, and epigenetics 11–12
Mike 86–87
mindfulness activities 43, 51
misbehaviour 36, 102, 156; *see also* behaviours
mistakes, making 53
Myers, Charles 78

National Literacy Strategy 180
Negative Thinking Patterns 7–8, 9; *see also* Automatic Negative Thoughts
nervous system **60**, 87; and behaviours 35, 140–41; and emotions 45; and fear 63; and safety 59, 143–44; and trust **53**; *see also* human brains
neuroception 89–90, 96–97
neuroscience 2, 17, 20, 25, 59, 63–64, 97, 101, 126, 148
noradrenaline **65**
novice teachers 14–16

Obama, Barack, on change 1
offences 131–32
Office for Standards in Education (Ofsted) 18, 26, 176–78, 182–83; and behaviour management 27–29
organisation **60**, 120
Oxytocin 59, **60**

parents 154–55
peace 164
pencil poem 49
permanent exclusions 19–20, 50, 93, 95, 104, 108, 111, 167, 178–79; and Ofsted 28–29; *see also* exclusion

Perry, Bruce 108
person-first language 127–28
planning **60**
polyvagal theory 59, 87–88
Porges, Stephen 87, 89
positive framing 143
post-traumatic stress disorder (PTSD) 78, 80; *see also* complex post-traumatic stress disorder
poverty 174–76, 179
Pratchett, Terry 184
"problem" boys, author teaching 4–6
process *vs.* theory 145
Progress 8 scores 175–76, 183
"PSHE Emotional Curriculum" 104, 117; relationship skills 121–22; responsible decision making 122–23; self-awareness 118–21; self-management 119–20
Pupil Premium 162
"Pupil Profile Tool" (PPT) 102, 104, 111, 117, 123, 152; and ACEs 105–06; and attachment theory 109–10; risk behaviours 108–09; and stress 106–07
Pupil Referral Units (PRUs) 180–81
Pupil Teachers' and Scholarship School Management (Flux) 21

questions 30–31; on guiding principles 55

rats, and epigenetics 11
reflection 156, 158–59
reflective thinking 123
Relational Inclusion 3, 17, 25, 68, 82, 125–27, 163, 165–67; and emotions 46; misconceptions about **47**; origins of 4–6; principles of 33–34; training for 180, 184
Relationalists 2
Relationally Inclusive "lenses" 70
relational policies 171
relationship building 10, 15, 18, 146–47; staff struggles with 62
relationship processes 40

relationships 36–37, **53–54**, 126, 139, 163; and avoidant attachment 92–93; with nature 73; with ourselves 40–41; staff relationships 38; student perspectives on 37
relationship skills 121–22
repairing 51–52, **54**, 151–52, 154, 159
repeat offenders 133
resilience 92–93
response flexibility 80
responsible decision making 122–23
restorative conversations 52, 145–46
restorative justice 162
Rhodesia 90
risk behaviours 108–09, *116*, 117
road rage 86
Robbins, Mel 56
Roberts, Luke 135, 147, 164–65
Romanian orphans 78–80
rules 170; *vs.* expectations 153–54; lack of clarity on 53, 149–50;

safety 75, 157–58; and disruptive behaviours 59; and learning 58; neuroscience of 59; student perceptions of 37–38, 45, 53, **53–54**
Santayana, George 78
School Quality Index 176
school readiness 77, 181–82
schools 101; autonomy of 173–74; beliefs about 77; importance of cultural fit to 38–40, 160, 167, 170; inclusive 126, 139, 173–74, 179, 183; and initiatives 162–63; inspections 26–30, 177–78; language used in 130–36; mainstream *vs.* segregated 23, 178; and mental health 178–80, 182, 184; needed system changes for 98, 164; policies 162–63; policing 134–35; problem issues 2; staff relationships 38; struggling 1–2; student perspectives on 37; training plans 169–70; transitions between 181–82, 184; uniforms 77; vision 168–69; and zero-tolerance policies 18–20
"The School Where Teachers Never Shout at Children" (BBC) 14
SEAL *see* Social and Emotional Aspects of Learning
sel-control/impulse control **60**, 120
self-awareness 42, 118–21
self-efficacy 118
self-management 119–20
self-monitoring **60**
self-reflection 145
self-regulation 43, 61, 129, 133, 153–54, 158; teaching 35, 42, 45; *see also* co-regulation
Serotonin 59, **60**
shame/humiliation, as child management tactic 21–22
shell shock 78
shouting, as classroom management 13–15, 18
Siegel, Dan 44, 142, 144
Social and Emotional Aspects of Learning (SEAL) 24–25
social engagement 87–88, 96–97, 158
social norms 121
somatic anxiety 114
"so what?" question 111, 129; and ACEs 112; hyperarousal 115; risk behaviours 117; stress 113–14
special needs children, and the Warnock Report 22–23
Spielman, Amanda 28
staff: behaviours of 62–63; code of conduct 169; dysregulated 52, 68, 129, 151; expectations of 152; induction processes for 170; and leadership 71, 165–66; mapping windows of trauma 70–71; and policies 167–68; reflection 96–97, 166; and Relational Inclusion 180; relationship-building struggles 62; safe places for 44; and self-reflection 145; training plans 169–70; *see also* teachers
staff recruitment 30–31
stepped approaches to behaviour 157–59

Still Face Experiment 83
stress 104, *113*, 114; de-escalating 157–58; positive 82; and the PPT 106–07; tolerable 82; toxic 83, 104
"Stress" Hormones **65**, 69
students: behavioural changes in 103; corporal punishment of 81–82; daily check-ins 71–72; exempted from accountability 174–75; lost children 102; mental health 178–80, 182; reasonable adjustments for 172, 177–78; and Relational Inclusion 166–67; shaming 21–22, **47**, 53, 86, 124, 133, 139–40, 146, 149–50, 154, 159; teacher attitudes towards 16, 101
sunflower lanyards 98
"Support for Learning" areas 171
survival instincts 7–8, 64
survival mode 35–36, **64**
suspensions 19–20, 152, 156, 167
Szekely, Louis 160

"talking with empathy" 143
task initiation **60**
teachers: building confidence of 147; code of conduct 169; communicating 122; demand for 67; early career 16, 64–65, 72–73; as entertainers 57–58; "everyone remembers" 57; facial expressions 89–90; fight or flight responses 69; induction processes for 170; and lack of empathy 62; mapping windows of trauma 70–71; novice 14–17; and policies 167–68; responsibilities 139–40; and rules 53, 149–50; students fearing 61; training plans 169–70; working with challenging behaviours 52; *see also* staff
teaching, as career choice 56–57, 68–69
technical language 126

Thatcher, Margaret 22
theatres 98
theory *vs.* process 145
Thomson, Dave 176
Three Bees 153–54
time 157, 160
time management **60**
trauma 64, 84–85, 98, 106, 125–26; and brain development 79–80, 97; case studies 86–87; family 155; vicarious trauma 70
trauma-informed approaches 33, 62, 80, 145
Tronick, Ed 83
Turecki, Jillian 74–75
Tutu, Desmond 7, 76

values 168–69
vandalism 133
van der Kolk, Bessell 114
Victorian England: and behaviours 34–35, 141; education in 20–21, 30–31; and emotions 45

Wagner, Stephi 11
walkie-talkies 134–35
walls 13
Warnock Committee/Report 22–24, 179
whole-class punishments 36
Wilson, Edward O. 73
windows of tolerance 44, 52, 129–30; mapping 70–71
WINE 143
Winfrey, Oprah 108
"withdrawal units" 171–72
witness statements 135–36
words 125, 127
working memory **60**
World War I 78
World War II 10

Yeats, W. B. 1

zero-tolerance policies 18–19, 77, 134, 140–41, 167
Zones of Regulation 45

For Product Safety Concerns and Information please contact our EU
representative GPSR@taylorandfrancis.com
Taylor & Francis Verlag GmbH, Kaufingerstraße 24, 80331 München, Germany

www.ingramcontent.com/pod-product-compliance
Lightning Source LLC
Chambersburg PA
CBHW070316240426
43661CB00057B/2659